DESTROYING THE DRUIDS ON MONA

Druids or Celtic priests from a print in 1868

Destroying the Druids on Mona

AD 60 & AD 78

Martin Williams

First publication: 2023

ISBN: 978–1-84524-518-4

Cover design: Lynwen Jones

Published by Gwasg Carreg Gwalch,
12 Iard yr Orsaf, Llanrwst, Wales LL26 0EH
tel: 01492 642031
email: books@carreg-gwalch.cymru
website: www.carreg-gwalch.cymru

Printed and published in Wales

To Sheila, Jason and Jonathan

Druidical remains in Anglesey

Acknowledgements

I would like to thank Jenny Stott for by piquing my interest about the Druids on Mona and putting me on the path of discovery. To Sían for keeping me straight with my spelling and grammar. To my great friend and countryman, both Portmadoc boys, Nev Pritchard who helped me with all things Welsh and translations. To all at Gwasg Carreg Gwalch who have been so helpful in getting this together.

I have had the pleasure of reading many pieces of work about this time period and its people by eminent, distinguished and learned people whose works made the picture of this age clearer.

Unless indicated below, photographs, maps and diagrams are by the author.

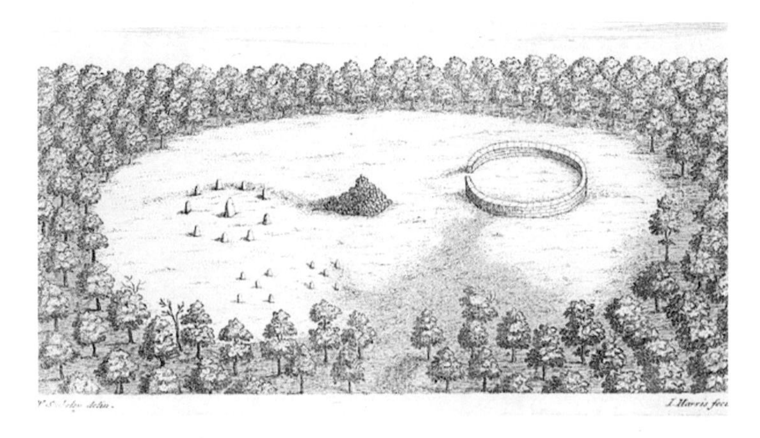

The great temple & grove of the druids
Tre'r Dryw in Anglesey

Contents

Introduction

Anglesey – Ynys Môn – is an island locatated on the north west coast of Wales which its inhabitants and visitors see as a quiet backwater known for its farming and tourism. There are 176 miles of coastline with many bays and sandy beaches enjoyed by hoards of visiting holiday makers.

Yet this seemingly quiet life belies the millenia of conflict and destruction that ravaged this island from all manner of invaders from a time going back to AD 60 with the Romans, followed by raids from the Irish, Danes and Vikings, the Normans, the English and Edward 1 and by Owain Glyndŵr's struggle for an independent Wales in 1400. The Normans and the English Kings wanted dominion over the land and an oath of fealty from the Welsh Kings and Princes' to the English crown. For the Danes and Vikings it was a source of goods, slaves and staging posts for their ships around the Irish Sea. The Irish either raided for goods and slaves or took the land to settle for themselves.

As for Rome, it was a much more than land and ownership, it was their military history that needed avenging. It was the Roman legions that brought about the most detructive and murderous acts of violence and barbarity upon the island's inhabitants in order to destroy a culture that had existed in communities in Britain and western Europe for centuries and that apparently was so despised by Roman generals.

There is little documentary evidence in the classical texts to explain why, how and where the Roman forces attacked through mainland Wales. There is no evidence whatsoever that the Roman Navy was active in the waters around North Wales; their activities seem to have been centred on cross channel sailings keeping this part of the Roman empire supplied with what it required.

Classical accounts of the Roman attacks of Mona, as they called the island, by both Gaius Seutonius Paulinus (AD 60) and Gnaeus Julius Agricola (AD 78) were described by the Roman historians Tacitus and Cassius Dio at least 20 years after the event...anecdotal writings based on the memories of individuals who were there, and short on facts!

Relevant information from Tacitus' *Annals* is missing – Books 7, 8, 9,10 and part of 11 are presumed lost (they covered the period between AD 37 and 47). The information held in them would have filled in some of the important gaps in our knowledge of this period. It could also have given us some insight into the reasons why the Druids were so detested by the Romans and they would seek their destruction.

The attacks on Mona were apparently to 'neutralize' the Druids and the subjugation of the 'resistance fighters'. The island was believed to be the 'heart' and training centre for the Druid culture for Britannia and Gaul. What was it that the Romans feared so much? The classical narrative is a 'one-sided' account, Celtic history and traditions were passed on orally through the generations, so there are no actual written records of their lives, religion, battles (with local tribes or 'invaders') or other events from their perspective. It is also quite probable that the savage and brutal actions of the Roman troops at the time may well have virtually annihilated many of the tribes who carried on the resistance, leaving no voices to 'tell the tale of...'. As has always been true throughout history, it is the victor who writes the story... which may not always be the whole truth or factually correct!! This book will offer up some possible answers to these questions based on what little physical archeological evidence has been uncovered so far and from written texts by Roman and Greek historians of the period and its aftermath. To try and follow the sequence events that prompted Roman action against the island. Sadly there is no written word from the inhabitants of the island or the lands adjacent, their's was an oral based culture of knowledge and traditions, many bourne in bardic poetry lost and diluted over time.

The actions of the Roman armies would have an impact on the people of Wales for a thousnad years. Great leaders would be born out of adversity on this island. From those roots would come the birth of a nation that would never be destroyed, its language, culture and history would remain to this day.

In order to gain a full picture of why these Roman miltary actions came about it is necessary to look at all the elements involved both on and off the island leading up to the fateful events that would rain down on its people and culture.

Martin Williams: 2023

Imaginative illustration of 'An Arch Druid in His Judicial Habit'

The Druids inciting the Brythonic warriors to oppose the landing of the Romans

An Island Of Many Names

The first recorded name that can be identified to this island is from classical texts during the Roman occupation of Britain in the 1st Century AD where the Roman historian Tacitus records it as **Mona Insulis** (*Mona Islands*) and from the second map, *Prima.Europa.Tabula*, created by Ptolomy in the 2nd century AD he identifies it as **Mona**.

From that time on, the historical texts have noted many names but none of which can be accurately dated or translated accurately (the Welsh has been anglicised or possibly misspelt):

Ynys Dowyll / Ynys Dywyll (*Old Welsh*): 'Black' or 'Dark Island' possibly referring to its history of the Druids and their 'ceremonial' groves.

Ynys Dewr: Island of the Brave

Clas Myrddin[1] / **Cae Myrddin**: Merlin's Enclosure

Y Fêl Ynys[1] / **Fêl Ynys:** The honey island

Ynys Brut[1] / **Ynys Bwyd**: Island of Food or Victuals

Onglisey/Ongullsey (*Old Norse*) *Translated as* Ongulls Island. During the 9th and 10th Centuries AD when it used

---

[1] *'Authentic Documents of Ancient British History'* Mr Urban, Paper IV, Jan 14th, The Gentlemans Magazine and Historical Chronicle, Vol 59 for the year 1789, Part the First, by Sylvanus Urban, London, Printed by John Nicholls, pp 30 -31

[1] *'Druidism of Ancient Britain'*, The New Church Repository and Monthly Review, Vol 1 No.7, July 1848, New York published by John Allen

as a landing/supply island for the Norsemen and Danes who were raiding and criss-crossing the Hibernian Sea.

Anglesey: Onglisey would be anglicised to this name around the time of the Norman incursions into the region during the 11th and 12th Centuries, and yet to the local people it would remain as Môn or Ynys Môn.

Môn Mam Cymru: (*Môn Mother Of Wales*) an epithet given to the island by Giraldus Cambrensis (12th century Archdeacon of Brecon) in his book ***'Descripto Cambriae'*** as it was deemed to be the 'bread basket of Wales' such was its ability to grow and provide food to the rest of Wales.

Looking over Lafan sands

The Known History of the Island

The island is situated on the north western coast of mainland Wales, separated from mainland Wales by the Menai Strait, is known to have been inhabited by humans as far back as the Neolithic period of the Stone age. The presence today of many standing stones, cromlechs, carnedds, monuments, hut circles, hill forts, enclosures and burial chambers that dot the landscape attest to that, with archaeological evidence showing that there has been human activity on the island going back some 4000 years.

Yet we have no knowledge of the individuals that peopled this place; how they lived their lives, the size of communities, their culture or even what gods they worshipped. The evidence of their existence, apart from these structures, is in their death rituals, how they were buried or cremated and the goods that went with them into their tombs/graves/pits. Yet even this is incomplete there is clear evidence that there were periods when no graves/tombs were dug and that cremation took place.

At Llyn Cerrig Bach (close to Holy Island on the west coast of Mona) in 1943, during the construction of RAF Valley, a hoard of 150 bronze and iron artefacts was found in the small lake and are believed to be votive offerings (tributes to the gods). Dating showed that these items included weapons, shields, chariots, slave chains and tools which spanned a period of 250 years up to the 1st Century AD.

The stone structures (standing stones, carnedd's, tombs etc.) that are spread about the island even today are of the greatest significance in that the concentration of these structures on the island is far greater here than anywhere else in Britain. In addition, according to local records state that a number of other structures did exist but were lost over time either by erosion or demolition due changes in the use of the land. It raises the question, what was so significant about this island that would have held it in such reverence and indeed considering the size of some of these structures what was the size of the population. Items found in excavated burials mounds show than they came from much further than the mainland in fact they appear to show that trading was occurring not only east to west but north to south as far as the Iberian peninsula. Finds from grave sites across the island dating from the Early Bronze Age (2000-1500 BC) are indicative of goods found as far south as the Iberian peninsula.

Finds from this time period grave sites are also indicative of goods found in the Low Countries and the Rhineland suggesting immigrants (e.g the Beaker people) settling here. Items recovered from burial sites containing cinerary urns along with incense urns and palstaves (bronze axes) date from the Middle Bronze age that suggest there was a new culture present on the island, as there were no graves have been found that date to this period. The island appears to have had an evolving and fluid population coming in via sea or the mainland. Considering there are only three ports on the island (Holyhead, Amlwch and Beaumaris) it was a busy place. It should be stated that there are a number of sandy bays both on the NW and SE coasts that could have had craft hauled up onto the shore.

The 1937 Survey and Inventory by the Royal Commission on Ancient and Historical Monuments in Wales and Monmouthshire indicates that the concentration of human settlement pre Roman Invasion of Britannia was predominantly along the Menai Strait and the NE part of the island. Advances in archaeological techniques and the discovery of parch marks have led to further discoveries of

Romans murdering Druids and burning their groves

structures across the island and next to the Strait; some with no datable evidence and others from the early Roman period.

In 2006 an aerial survey observed a large earthworks just south of Amlwch. A three day archaeological investigation was carried out by Channel 4's Time Team in 2007 but they found little evidence to indicate who occupied it, though they did consider the structure to be a hill fort dating to the 1st Century AD and not of Roman construction. We do know that there were periods of human migration from Europe into Britain from 500 BC onwards due to pressure from populations from further east. There are no written texts or even textual carvings from this period so we are reliant on the limited items found in burials and cremation pits to give us an indication of the movement of specific tribes who can be attributed these specific wares. Given the limited data spread over the centuries we cannot identify the group or groups (and there culture) who were inhabiting the island before the Romans arrived in Britain. There are identifiable hill forts on the island that may indicate a sizeable population and there are small forts mainly on the coastline, suggesting these may have been used in time of necessity (a refuge from raiders). Concentrations of dwellings that could be identified were close to the Menai Strait and along the NE coast but there may have been more as this was more than likely an agrarian society and most of their dwellings may well not have been substantial enough to leave an 'imprint' millennia later. At best it would be a shot in the dark guess as to the population size.

The land is relatively low lying and fertile (compared with the mountainous mainland of North Wales) with hills spaced evenly over the north of the island, the highest recorded is Holyhead Mountain at 220m (720 ft) on Holy

Island. There are a few natural lakes, the largest being Llyn Llywenan: 1.1 km long and 0.4 km wide, slightly smaller are Llyn Coran and Llyn Traffwll. The streams and rivers run predominantly north east to south west as does much of the topography of the island.

The climate is humid (unlike the mainland which tends to be much wetter due to the influence of the Snowdonia Mountain range) and the growing season is earlier than the mainland because of its more moderate climate. Much of the inland areas of the island are covered by permeable boulder clays, alluvial and glacial silts, sands and gravels utilised over the millenia for producing arable crops, hence the epithet of Mam Cymru (*Mother of Wales*) given to the island by Giraldus Cambrensis.

Today the ancient woodland only covers approximately 0.5% of the island[1] and is located primarily along the Menai Strait the eastern coastline. It was noted in the 1937 Survey and Inventory by the RCAHMWM that samples of carbonised wood and nuts found at Bryn-yr-Hen-Bobl (a chambered cairn) near Plas Newydd, showed the predominance of Oak (sessile/common) followed by Hazel, Hawthorn and smaller samples of Maple, Birch, Ash, Alder and Willow. Sycamore was also in evidence. This sampling was believed to be a fair representation of the tree population that had existed in ancient times in areas where the underlying boulder clays would accommodate tree growth. There are areas to the north, and west of the island where the underlying schist rock is near the surface and where only scrub could survive. They also found Scots Pine in a post hole at Bryn Celli Ddu. Clearly far more woodland was present in ancient times. It is important to determine

[1] *'Based on information in Anglesey County Council Report on the Anglesey's Tree, Hedgerow and Woodland Strategy*, 2003-2008

the presence of the tree types that would have been present on the island as they do play a part in the islands violent history of the Roman period.

The only mineral resource on the island is the copper from Parys Mountain, in the north of the island, which is believed to have been mined since the Bronze age.

The Menai Strait which separates Mona from the mainland is 25 km (16 miles) long from Fort Belan in the south west to Beaumaris in the north east. Its width at Low Water ranges from over 1,000m to approximately 300m around Moel y Don. There are large sandbars and mudflats between Fort Belan and Porth Dinorwig, Felinheli. The narrows then continue up to the Swellies and then start to open out towards the vast Lafan Sands beyond Bangor and Beaumaris. The Strait experiences a two way tidal surges on every tide (dealt with in more depth in a later chapter).

Prior to the construction of the Menai Suspension Bridge by Thomas Telford in 1826, the main ferry crossing was from Porthaethwy (*Port of the Daethwy, believed to have been a local Celtic tribe*) on Mona, to Bangor (mainland) at the north east end of the Strait (one of the narrowest parts of the Strait). There is at least one historical record recounting the loss of a full herd of cattle being driven across the Strait (even with drovers in boats on both sides of the herd to keep them in a direct line) due to the 'treacherous currents' – some of the worst around Britain. Pigs were also driven over at this point to the mainland and would rest on a small island called Ynys y Moch, 'island of pigs' before swimming the rest of the way across. This small island is now the base for the bridge support on the Anglesey side and is clearly visible at low tide. Just to the SW of the bridge is an area known to sailors for many millenia as the Swellies, where underwater shoals and rocks create whirlpools (the well known one being Pwll Ceris) and rapid currents make it one

Bryn-Celli-Ddu

Bryn-yr-Hen-Bobl

Eisteddfod stone circle near Menai Bridge

Maen Llandegfan

Maen Hir Mona

Penrhos Feilw standing stones

Cromlech Llansadwrn

Llanfair-is-gaer

Moel y Don

of the most dangerous areas of the Strait. Theoretically it is possible to ford the Strait here at low water on a spring tide when the depth may fall to 0.5m BUT the current runs at about 4.8 knots making it extremely difficult. Is is reasonable to suggest that ferry services may have been in existence between the island and the mainland there are much later records of them between Porthaethwy (Menai Bridge) and Bangor, Llanidan and Llanfair-is-gaer, Moel y Don and Porth Dinorwig, Felinheli. How and when these were first established is not known but they were used for centuries so it is not unreasonable to assume that as good crossing points they would have been used as early as the 1st Century AD and even further back than that.

Trade between the island and the mainland would have benefited both. We do know that gold from the Wicklow Mountains in Ireland did come through Mona and on into the mainland in the 1st century. There are records that show the Greeks were trading along the coast of Britannia in the 4th Century BC; the Greek geographer Pytheas of Massilia[1] (a Greek trading port established in the western Mediterranean) had explored the coastline presumably also looking for trading opportunities. How do the inhabitants of Mona connect with mainland Europe and the wrath of the Roman Empire? History tends to paint a 'broad stroke' when it comes to identifying the peoples that occupied central and western Europe. Roman ethnography in the 1st Century BC classed the zones on the western European mainland area as Gallia Celitca (the largest zone in middle and western France), Gallia Belgica (northern France and Belgium), Gallia Cisalpina (Alpine region of France), Gallia Nabonesis (what is now SE France) and Gallia Aquitania (SW France) but when the Gallic wars with

---

[1] *Known today as Marseilles*

Porth Amlwch

Fort Belan

Rome commenced it was against the Gauls (all the zones were classed together). It is likely that the Celts in Europe had no shared identity (they would not have considered themselves Celtic) but may have had similar customs and possibly a comparable language

Living as separate tribes in villages and small towns but certainly having no cities comparable to those of Greece and Rome. The Iron Age Britons, despite never being referred to as Celts in ancient literature (Roman and Greek historians identified then by their tribal names) are often included in studies of the Celts by modern scholars based on the similarities in language, culture, farming and art found in Britannia and in continental Europe. So the term Celt for the 'native' population in Britannia has also to be broad based, and it is possible that not all the tribes shared the same culure to the immigrants from the continent.

The immigration of these 'Celtic communities' from Europe brought new farming ideas and tools which would have had an impact in the areas they settled in (which were primarily the soil rich lands of the south east and the Midlands). They would have been slow to migrate to the poorer mountainous lands to the west or to the island itself. The Britannic mainland population density during this period would have been increasing not only because the the 'newcomers' but also because of increased food production due to improved farming techniques in the more fertile crop producing low-lying southern and midland areas areas of Britannia. So there may have well been growing diversity between these poulations and those of the south west, west and north. There does appear to be a greater number of different tribes in the mid and southern areas than the rest of Britannia from the information that we do have.

The west and the north were prediminantly mountainous and would have been less affected by these farming practices as the land was of a poorer quality therfore livestock farming would have been more predominant. Based on current archaeological evidence we have of Mona it does not seem to have been a viable proposition of invasion for profit. Arable production would not have been at levels that were being produced in south eastern Britannia and the copper extraction was believed to be on a small scale. Neither were there any major harbours only small trading ports. The one exception may have been as a source of plunder and slaves taken by raiders to be sold in the markets of Ireland, Britannia or beyond.

Authors note: In recent years historians have challenged the term Celtic as being the correct name for a specific population of western Europe (and beyond to the east) during this period. The belief now is that 'Celtic' is an all-encompassing name used to describe tribes who shared a common cultural style and a similar language; as recorded by the ancient historians of Rome and Greece. Wherever possible in this narrative the tribal peoples will be described in terms of the name the Romans attributed to them, though it is likely some of these may have been generalised and included smaller tribes that co-existed in the same region.

It should also be made clear that the term 'Celtic' regarding Britannia and Hibernia refers to those nations speaking Irish, Scottish Gaelic, Manx and Welsh (as descibed by Edward Lhuyd - ref page 65 - in his study of these languages which also included Breton of western France).

The Coming of the Romans

The Romans believed that Britannia and Hibernia (Ireland) were at the 'edge of the known world', therefore any cultural changes, new farming systems and tools, building and metallurgical techniques would be slower to develop at the 'fringes'. Any changes would have relied on the movement of 'skilled people' migrating westwards and taking with them new ideas and 'educating' the local population. In some small way it is likely that trade and contact with 'europeans' would have had some influence on the coastal tribes.

The first Roman troops to land on the island of Britannia came with Caesar in 55 BC not to invade but to cut off supplies to the Gallic tribes he was fighting in western Europe. Many of the tribes-people who had migrated from their tribal lands in Europe to create a new life in Britannia still retained links with their homeland (for example the Atrebates from Belgica into the south east Britannia) and would have come to their aid when the Roman 'war machine' advanced to take their homeland and sell their tribes-people into slavery. The local Britannic tribes were well aware that the Romans were coming and were waiting for them as a united front however this first incursion was no more than a beach head landing as the weather conspired against Caesar as severe storms damaged his fleet and he had to return to Gaul.

A year later he was back, more organised this time, and immediately advanced some 19 km (12 miles) through the dark and met up with the Britannia forces at a river crossing (believed to be a section of the river Stour in Kent). The tribes were beaten back and re-grouped further inland but were beaten again. While planning to move his troops further forward to take advantage of the situation Julius Caesar received word that bad weather had severely damaged his fleet again. So once again he pulled his legions back in order to deal with the situation. According to Caesar (in his books *Commentarii de Bello Gallico*) this time he remained at the coast and built a fortified camp to protect his troops and where he could repair his ships.

Within the year he returned to battle and found that that the tribes had amassed a combined forceagainst him led by Cassivellaunus (tribal chief of the *Catuvellauni*). This tribal chief was looking to become the dominant force in southern Britannia before the Romans had arrived. He had recently overthrown the king of the *Trinovantes* tribe and forced the king's son (Mandubracius) into exile - he had actually gone to the Romans in Gaul requesting help to get his kingdom back, and must have been with Caesars forces when they landed. After several (failed) frontal assaults against the Roman Legions it became clear to Cassivellaunus that he could not defeat the Roman troops in direct battle so after disbanding his main force, he proceeded to use guerilla tactics and the mobility of his vast number of war chariots to slow the Roman advance. The Romans proved to be an unstoppable 'machine' they continued their advance and reached the banks of the Thames, the border into the *Catuvellauni* territory. It was here that he met envoys from the *Trinovantes* tribe who offered Caesar aid and provisions if he would restore Mandubracius as their king. This he agreed to do and was supplied with grain and hostages (considered a valuable asset) – note: Caesar states in his writings that five other tribes acceded to the Romans at this time: the *Cenimagni, Segontiacti, Ancalites, Bibroci and the Cassi* – the location of these tribes is not known. From these new 'friends' Caesar was able to determine where Cassivellaunus' stronghold

(Verulamium) was, and besieged it.

Even though Cassivellaunus requested help from other tribes their actions did not affect the outcome and he surrendered to Caesar. No land was taken by the Romans. The *Trinovantes* land was returned to them and their new King, Mandubracius, would remain friendly to Rome. As for the *Catuvellauni* chieftain, he had to undertake not to attack the *Trinovantes*, hand over hostages to Caesar and pay an annual tribute to Rome (though in fact, it was probably never paid). Further Roman incursions into Britannia did not occur as news reached Caesar that growing unrest amongst the tribes in Gaul was building again, so he left with his Legions and hostages before the coming winter, never to return.

During his whole Gallic campaign Caesar had recorded a great many observations of the tribes he had encountered in mainland Europe and Britannia, which would have a major impact on Britannia, and subsequently Mona, in the future as Rome itself set its eyes on the 'soft prize' of Britannia. He noted their capacity and ability for batttle, their culture, their wealth in farming and metals and their religious community. This information was collated into his book 'Commentarii De Bello Gallico' and may well have been used as a basis by future Emperors in their plans of expansion into Britannia. There are a number of observations that he does make about a religious group called the Druids who he first encounters in Europe and who appeared to have played a significant part in tribal life, politics and judicial decisions of the tribal leaders. The following extracts are from a translation[1] of the book, and in these we have the first insights as to who these Druids

[1] C. Julius Caesar. Caesar's Gallic War. *Translator*. W. A. McDevitte. Translator. W. S. Bohn. 1st Edition. New York. Harper & Brothers. 1869. Harper's New Classical Library.

were and what impact they would have on the events to come for the island of Mona Insulis and its inhabitants.

Caesar, Commentarii De Bello Gallico, Book 6 .13

'Throughout all Gaul there are two orders of those men who are of any rank and dignity: for the commonality is held almost in the condition of slaves, and dares to undertake nothing of itself, and is admitted to no deliberation. The greater part, when they are pressed either by debt, or the large amount of their tributes, or the oppression of the more powerful, give themselves up in vassalage to the nobles, who possess over them the same rights without exception as masters over their slaves. But of these two orders, one is that of the Druids, the other that of the knights. The former are engaged in things sacred, conduct the public and the private sacrifices, and interpret all matters of religion. To these a large number of the young men resort for the purpose of instruction, and they [the Druids] *are in great honor among them. For they determine respecting almost all controversies, public and private; and if any crime has been perpetrated, if murder has been committed, if there be any dispute about an inheritance, if any about boundaries, these same persons decide it; they decree rewards and punishments; if any one, either in a private or public capacity, has not submitted to their decision, they interdict him from the sacrifices. This among them is the most heavy punishment. Those who have been thus interdicted are esteemed in the number of the impious and the criminal: all shun them, and avoid their society and conversation, lest they receive some evil from their contact; nor is justice administered to them when seeking it, nor is any dignity bestowed on them. Over all these Druids one presides, who possesses supreme authority among them. Upon his death, if any individual among the rest is pre-eminent in dignity, he succeeds; but, if there are many equal, the election is made by the suffrages of the Druids; sometimes they even contend for the presidency with arms. These*

assemble at a fixed period of the year in a consecrated place in the territories of the Carnutes, which is reckoned the central region of the whole of Gaul. Hither all, who have disputes, assemble from every part, and submit to their decrees and determinations. This institution is supposed to have been devised in Britain, and to have been brought over from it into Gaul; and now those who desire to gain a more accurate knowledge of that system generally proceed thither for the purpose of studying it.'

Caesar, Commentarii De Bello Gallico, Book 6.14

'The Druids do not go to war, nor pay tribute together with the rest; they have an exemption from military service and a dispensation in all matters. Induced by such great advantages, many embrace this profession of their own accord, and [many] are sent to it by their parents and relations. They are said there to learn by heart a great number of verses; accordingly some remain' in the course of training twenty years. Nor do they regard it lawful to commit these to writing, though in almost all other matters, in their public and private transactions, they use Greek characters. That practice they seem to me to have adopted for two reasons; because they neither desire their doctrines to be divulged among the mass of the people, nor those who learn, to devote themselves the less to the efforts of memory, relying on writing; since it generally occurs to most men, that, in their dependence on writing, they relax their diligence in learning thoroughly, and their employment of the memory. They wish to inculcate this as one of their leading tenets, that souls do not become extinct, but pass after death from one body to another, and they think that men by this tenet are in a great degree excited to valor, the fear of death being disregarded. They likewise discuss and impart to the youth many things respecting the stars and their motion, respecting the extent of the world and of our earth, respecting the nature of things, respecting the power and the majesty of the immortal gods'.

Caesar, Commentarii De Bello Gallico, Book 6.16

'The nation of all the Gauls is extremely devoted to superstitious rites; and on that account they who are troubled with unusually severe diseases, and they who are engaged in battles and dangers, either sacrifice men as victims, or vow that they will sacrifice them, and employ the Druids as the performers of those sacrifices; because they think that unless the life of a man be offered for the life of a man, the mind of the immortal gods can not be rendered propitious, and they have sacrifices of that kind ordained for national purposes. Others have figures of vast size, the limbs of which formed of osiers they fill with living men, which being set on fire, the men perish enveloped in the flames. They consider that the oblation of such as have been taken in theft, or in robbery, or any other offense, is more acceptable to the immortal gods; but when a supply of that class is wanting, they have recourse to the oblation of even the innocent.'

Caesar, Commentarii De Bello Gallico, Book 6.17

'They worship as their divinity, Mercury in particular, and have many images of him, and regard him as the inventor of all arts, they consider him the guide of their journeys and marches, and believe him to have great influence over the acquisition of gain and mercantile transactions. Next to him they worship Apollo, and Mars, and Jupiter, and Minerva; respecting these deities they have for the most part the same belief as other nations: that Apollo averts diseases, that Minerva imparts the invention of manufactures, that Jupiter possesses the sovereignty of the heavenly powers; that Mars presides over wars. To him, when they have determined to engage in battle, they commonly vow those things which they shall take in war. When they have conquered, they sacrifice whatever captured animals may have survived the conflict, and collect the other things into one place. In many states you may see piles of these things heaped up in

their consecrated spots; nor does it often happen that any one, disregarding the sanctity of the case, dares either to secrete in his house things captured, or take away those deposited; and the most severe punishment, with torture, has been established for such a deed.'

Caesar, Commentarii De Bello Gallico, Book 6.18

'All the Gauls assert that they are descended from the god Dis, and say that this tradition has been handed down by the Druids. For that reason they compute the divisions of every season, not by the number of days, but of nights; they keep birthdays and the beginnings of months and years in such an order that the day follows the night. Among the other usages of their life, they differ in this from almost all other nations, that they do not permit their children to approach them openly until they are grown up so as to be able to bear the service of war; and they regard it as indecorous for a son of boyish age to stand in public in the presence of his father'.

It is clear, according to Caesar descriptions, that these Druids played a significant role within the tribal structure and influence with the tribal leaders in Europe and yet there 'institution' was devised somewhere in Britannia. What is not seen in these writings is any perceived threat to the Romans by these Druids, they appear to be just a part of the tribal culture and yet within 100 years that notion completely changes. changes.

It is highly probable that following Caesar's departure trading in all sorts of goods would have opened up even more between Britannia and mainland Europe and opportunities to expand their business as far as Caesar's homeland. Rome knew that tin, lead, copper and gold where being readily traded across the channel from Britannia and that it had a large population an attractive proposition to the leaders of Rome. Plans were made to invade Britannia again in 34 and 25 BC, but on each occasion revolts elsewhere in the empire prevented it from happening.

Meanwhile in Britannia, Cassivellaunus (King of the most powerful tribe in SE Britannia), believing that Rome would not be bothered with Britannia while it was dealing with issues elsewhere in its empire, and ignoring Caesar's orders to cease his own expansion plans began to increase his tribe's territory from its heartland north of the river Thames in all directions, building up the larger kingdom that will dominate south-east of the country for the next century and the one which adopts the *Catuvellauni* name.

In AD 40 and Emperor Gaius Caligula's attention was drawn to Britannia with the arrival of one of King Cunobeline's[1] sons (Adminius, exiled by his father) who persuaded Caligula that Britannia was ready for the taking. Since Caesar's landing's Rome had made many inroads in trade with Britannia and had allegiances with a few of the tribes (e.g. the *Atrebates, Canti* and the *Trinovantes*). Gaius had an army assembled at Boulogne ready to sail but a mutiny broke out amongst his legions – they refused to cross the water, no invasion took place. After Caligula was murdered in AD 41 Claudius became Emperor (and it is believed that in order to cement his position as emperor he must be 'seen' to bring new wealth to Rome. Britannia was seen as the better option, they had 'friends' there already. Tacitus[2] notes in his Annals *'Britannia permits and is even prolific of crops; they ripen slowly but are quick to sprout. She also produces gold, silver and other metals, conquest is*

---

[1] *Grandson of Cassivellanus and head of the Catuvellauni tribe and lands.*

[2] *There are a number of variations of translations of the works by Tacitus. For the most part and for consistency reference has been made to:* Annals *by Palatine Press,* Histories *by Oxford World Classics, and* Agricola *by Macmillan,1877, by Alfred John Church and William Jackson Brodribb.*

worthwhile'. It was a good source of grain and metals, and more importantly seemed to be at a state where in-fighting between the local tribes meant that it was unlikely that a large cohesive army could be brought against a Roman invasion. With much of the staff preparation already completed for Gaius Caligula the plans were set in motion for the Roman Legions to move on Britannia 'without too much cost' to the Roman coffers. Something Nero, Claudius' successor would continue 'paying the bill' for, when successive Governors of Britannia found it was not that easy to 'subdue the natives'

The Romans would be back on the shores of Britannia in AD 43 and this time they would be here to stay. Unlike Caesar's 55 BC incursion into southern Britain where he had been hindered by poor information on invasion sites and the strength of forces they may be up against, General Aulus Plautius on this occasion, made sure that he had as much up to date information as possible. However, as had happened when Caligula had his troops on the shore of Gaul ready to cross the Channel in AD 40 to invade Britain, his troops also refused to sail over. On this occasion though Plautius reacted by having monies brought from Rome to 'incentivise' the troops to sail across the Channel in 3 tranches and land on the coast of the *Canti* (Kent).

The Roman Legions that arrived on the British shores were seasoned veterans of many battles in Gaul and Germania, and had the advantage of superior weapons, armour and tactics, unlike the local tribes who appear to have won their battles against adjacent tribes by sheer strength in numbers. These Legions amounting to approximately 20,000 men were the:-

II Augusta,V1111 Hispana, X1111 Gemina and the XX Valeria

together with and approximately 20,000 Auxiliary troops.

Cohorts and cavalry (ala) of Batavians and Thracians are documented as being included in this force but little is known of the other forces with them.

On landing, the Roman Legions met no resistance, possibly because the 'British' tribes had received the news that the Romans had refused to cross the water and so had felt no need to set up defences. Only when they landed did Caratacus and Togodobnus (King Cunobeline's sons) react and rush warriors to meet the 'enemy'. The Romans passed through the land of the *Canti* tribe (in Kent) seemingly easily and eventually at the river Medway met a force made up of the *Catuvellauni* tribe and their supporters led by Caratacus and Togodubnus, beating them in open battle. Tacitus writes *'The physique of the people presents many varieties, whence inferences are drawn: the red hair and the large limbs of the Caledonians proclaim their German origin: the swarthy faces of the Silures, the curly quality in general of their hair and the position of Spain opposite their shores. Those peoples who adjoin Gaul are also like Gauls, their celebration of Gallic ceremonies and faith in Gallic superstitions, the language is not very different. The Britons display a higher spirit not having been emasculated by long years of peace* [*comparing them to the men of Gaul*]. *The strength lies in their infantry but certain tribes also fight from chariots; the driver has the place of honour, the combatants are merely retainers. Originally the people were subjected to kings, now they are distracted by parties and party spirits through the influence of chieftains but with no common purpose, rarely will 2 or 3 states confer to repulse a common enemy: accordingly they fight individually and are collectively conquered'*.

The defending forces fell back to the other side of the river Thames and waited for the Romans to cross, though they became lax in their watchfulness believing that the Romans had no bridge or boats with which to cross the river. It was now that the Roman general Aulus Paulitus used the skills of his Auxiliary forces (the Batavian's ability to swim a river in full armour – skills they had learnt in their homeland in the Rhine Delta). He had them cross in the dark, catching the tribes completely by surprise and fought them for 2 days until they were beaten (it was here that Togodubnus was killed in battle): the Roman tactics and skills proved overwhelming to the British tribes. Beaten but not defeated, Caratacus fled west with the remainder of his men to continue the fight first to the land of the *Dubonni* (though this tribe soon capitulated to the invading Roman army as they were not a war-like tribe) and then on to the land of the Silures and *Ordovices.*

Resistance in the south seems to have crumbled, some of the tribes were already in favour of Rome and the other tribes believed that for self-preservation it better to ally themselves with the Romans because they were not able to put up a challenge against the Roman forces. As can be seen from the timeline chart overleaf the tribes of the south and midlands came under Roman 'rule' within nine years. Some tribes had resisted longer than others buts the might of the Roman army and its tactics had prevailed. To the west and north many others sought to defend their island against these invaders. These 'rebellious' tribes knowing that they could not defeat the Romans in open battle decided to harass Roman troops using guerilla tactics. Caesar had noted that:

Caesar, Commentarii de Bello Gallico 4.33

'Their mode of fighting with their chariots is this; firstly they drive about in all directions and throw their weapons and generally break the ranks of the enemy with the very dread of their horses and the noise of their wheels; and when they have worked themselves in between the troops of horse, leap from their

chariots and engage on foot. The charioteers in the meantime, withdraw some little distance from the battle, and so place themselves with the chariots that, that, if their masters are overpowered by the number of the enemy, they may have a ready retreat to their own troops. Thus they display in battle the speed of the horse, [together with] the firmness of infantry; and by daily practice and exercise attain to such expertness that they are accustomed, even on a declining or steep place, to check their horses at full speed, and manage and turn them in an instant and run along the pole, and stand on the yoke, and thence betake themselves with the greatest celerity to their chariots again'.

It was clear that the Britons could not defeat these organised Roman troops in open battle, the battle tactics that the Britons had used so often against their local enemies were of no use. They could not break the impenetrable wall of'metal' and were losing too many good fighters, even their charioteers could not swing the course of the battle in their favour. These Romans knew these tactics as they were similar to those used against them by their 'cousins' across in Europe, it was a hard fight but they knew they could beat them. It became obvious to their leaders that Rome was going to crush them and the resistance began to crumble knowing that they would either die by the sword (or pilum) or surrender to the yoke of Roman rule.

Emperor Claudius and Rome wanted and believed the invasion of Britannia would be a short campaign, as it had been for Caesar in Gaul; what they did not want was a drawn out campaign that would drain the resources of Rome even further. So General Aulus Paulitus (and successive governors of Britannia) was under orders from the Emperor to bring the population under Roman rule as soon as possible. To this end, General Paulitus now began using the 'discord and animosity' that existed amongst the

Britannic tribes to his advantage. He invited Emperor Claudius to Britannia to join him in the 'final push' to defeat the Britons. Claudius arrived from Gessoriacum (Boulogne) with war elephants and heavy weapons and joined Plautius. At this point a number of tribes seeing that 'oining with Rome' may well be the best option, immediately met with Claudius and made treaties with him: the figure of 11 is quoted in many texts: certainly the Cantiaci, Atrebates (under Verica), Regni (under Togidubnus), Trinovantes, Iceni (under Antedius and Prasatugus), Brigantes (under Venutius and Cartimandua), Dobunni (under Bouocus) and possibly the Corielvati (both of the latter had been under pressure from the Catuvellauni) but the rest are unknown[1]. Relevant information from Tacitus' *Annals* (that covered the period between AD 37 and 47) is missing – Books 7, 8, 9,10 and part of 11 are presumed lost – the information held in them would have filled in some of the important gaps in our knowledge.

In all the historical texts of this time that have been researched there appears to be no mention of the presence of Druids either in the battle zones or at the meetings between the tribal chieftains and the Romans – something that surely would have been recorded had they been present at the meeting with Claudius.

The time line overleaf gives an indication of how the tribes of southern Britain (between Kent, Cornwall and Cheshire fell under the Roman occupation) their resistance had lasted some 9 years from the initial invasion. It should be stated that though it took 9 years, it was not 9 years of continuous fighting, most Roman military actions took place during their 'fighting season' (March to

[1] *The Coritani, Parisii, Belgae, Durotriges, Dumnonii, Dobunni and Conovii have been proposed in a number of academic books but some of these were still fighting Roman troops at the time of the meeting with Claudius.*

October), the troops would billet down in fortified camps during the winter when snow, ice and low temperatures would impede any action, but is also gave the 'enemy' a chance to regroup and train, the resistance was not over. The tribes to the west continued to harass the Romans and their allies using hit and run tactics under the leadership of Caratacus (Caradoc) and to the north there was an uneasy truce between the Roman Governor and the Brigantes whose lands stretched form the west coast to the east coast. Looking at the timeline chart it can be seen that Aulus Paulitus had conquered most of the lands south of the line between the Severn estuary and Lincoln by AD 47 (some 4 years after the initail landing). Then began the incursions into the lands of western Britannia while still trying to consolidate their hold to the east and south. This was not going to be an easy venture, they were now up against a determined enemy fighting in the mountains who knew the ground well and were well led.

What is not recorded in the classical texts is the presence of the Druids at any negotiations in peace talks with the tribes who were conquered or that they were involved, nor even any comment as to them being instrumental in whipping up the tribal resistance against Roman occupation, rule and their laws.

There is no mention of the Druids at all, which has us questioning why such severe actions would be taken against them by the Romans.

Time line: Subduing and Controlling of British Tribes by the Romans

Tribe	Location (as recognised today)	By AD	Governor
Cantiaci ^	Kent and part of Sussex	43	Aulus Plautius AD 43-47
Atrebates^	Hampshire, parts of Surrey and Sussex	43	
Regnenses^	Parts of Sussex and Surrey	43	
Trinovantes^	Parts of Essex and Suffolk	44	
Catuvellauni	Hertfordshire, Northamptonshire, Bedfordshire,Buckinghamshire,	44 – 46	
Belgae	Cambridgeshire and part of Essex	43 – 44	
Dubnunni	Parts of Hampshire, Wiltshire and Somerset	46	
Durotiges	Avon and parts of Gloucestershire	46	
Corieltauvi	Lincolnshire, Leicestershire, Rutland, Nottinghamshire, parts of Northamptonshire and parts of	46 – 47	Ostorius Scapula AD 47-52
Iceni^	Derbyshire	47	
Cornovii	Norfolk, Suffolk and Cambridgeshire	47	
	Cheshire, Shropshire, North Staffs and eastern parts of Flintshire, Powys and		
Deceangli	Wrexham	48	
Damnonii	Flintshire and Denbighshire	49 - 51	
Curatrixes*	Devon and parts of Somerset and Dorset	52	
	Cornwall, parts of Devon and Somerset		
Cornish Coronovii*		52	
	South west Cornwall and part of Devon		

^ *Allied with Romans from the outset of the invasion*

* *Believed to be sub-groups of the Dumnonii tribe*

Druids temple near Ilton

Wooded Ridge, Anglesey. The ridge, viewed here from the end, is covered in sycamores, but in pre-Roman Druidical times, perhaps they were sacred oaks

Western Britannia 1st Century AD

The map below is based on a map, PRIMA- EṼRO PE-TABṼLA, drawn by Ptolemy, a Greek geographer circa AD 150. It was of western Europe (though his source of information is unclear) and recorded the distribution of known tribes in Britain around AD 40. He may have referenced other maps of western Europe between 60 BC and AD 100 based on facts gained from various sources to show who was where and when but their accuracy may be questionable.

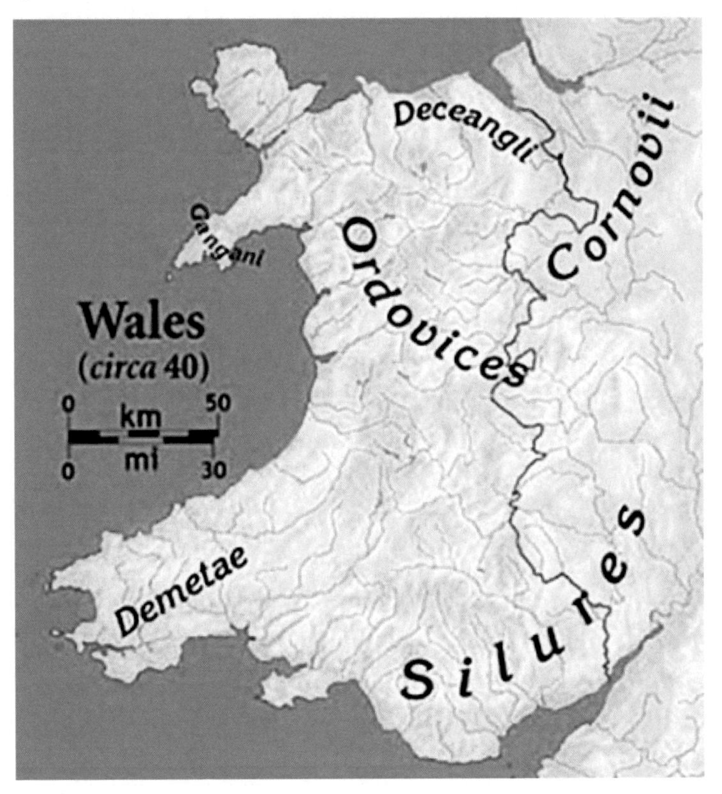

Wales (Circa 40) (Wikimedia Commons)

There was a line of vexillation forts, together with smaller forts along the 'frontier' with anti-Roman tribes from Glevum to Lindum defending the tribes 'under their protection'. The Roman construction of roads (Watling Street, Ermine Street and the Fosse Way) was commencing at a pace in order to be able to move supplies, troops and materials quickly from their main ports in the south.

Aulus Plautius' term of office as Governor of Britannia came to an end in AD 47, and he returned to Rome in full honour to celebrate being awarded an Ovation (a Roman triumph against an inferior enemy, but not in war, and there was little or no danger to the army itself) at which he wore a crown of Myrtle and walked before the people (without the army or the Senate for an escort). Through his work, using both military and political tactics, he had secured most of lowland zone Britannia for Rome and his Emperor.

However not all was at it seemed: Claudius and the Senate had believed that securing Britannia should have been relatively easy to do. As it turns out, because of the Roman way of dealing with situations and the resistance against accepting their rule, when the new Governor, Ostorius Scapula, arrived he found the 'frontier' in flames.

As Tacitus records it (*Annals* 12.31) *'the enemy had burst into the territories of our allies, imagining that with winter beginning the new governor would not march against them. However, he did use rapid movement of light cohorts and cut down all who opposed Ostorius Scapula and pursued all those who fled in order to prevent them rallying. He prepared to disarm all whom he suspected and occupy all the encampments in the whole country to the Avon and Severn'*. It is likely the 'enemy' were the *Silures* and *Ordovices* (led by Caratacus) on their neighbours the *Dobunnii*, and the *Decangli* on the *Cornovii.*

In order to secure his position in the rear and prior to campaigning in the west, Scapula decided on a 'Disarming policy' on those tribes that had voluntarily entered an alliance with Rome and who still held their weapons (as opposed to those who had fought, lost and been disarmed). This policy forbade the possession or arms except for hunting or self-defence on a journey. Needless to say, many members of the *Iceni* and *Corieltavi* tribes rebelled against the policy and took up arms. Scapula rapidly moved his forces against the rebels and defeated them. [Note: as Prasatugus did not take up arms he was placed in charge of all the Iceni to calm the region down - the fate of Antedius is not known].

From the *Silures* homeland (what we know now as the Welsh Marches of South Wales) up through Shropshire and the Cheshire Gap (under the control of the *Cornovii*) and on to the western confederation tribal land of the Brigantes, was a corridor that was being used as an 'escape route' for those wishing to continue to fight the Romans (or fired up by desperation of losing everything in the Roman advance). Scapula saw that he needed to close this gap so that there was no escape for the 'defeated' or a route for reinforcements from the north.

He now moved against the *Cornovii*[1] who occupied the land between the estuary of the river Dee and the headwaters of the river Trent. Much of the area was lowland forest and most of the tribe were concentrated in the southern part of their lands – Shropshire). He divided the

---

[1] *the Cornovii were the only Britannic tribe that were to eventually raise an auxiliary force for the Romans (the* **Cohors Primae Cornoviorum**) *and served in Britannia – the actual number of men is not known but a military cohort was normally 500 men.*

XIIII Legion into 2 vexillations: the northern section built forts at Letocetum and Pennocrucium, whilst the southern section built a fort at Leighton next to the *Cornovii* hill fort on the Wrekin. In a relatively short time they had conceded to the Roman forces as they saw them as a better option than constant raiding from the *Ordovices* and *Deceangli.*

Following this success it was now the turn of the *Deceangli.* Their tribal lands were on the north-east border of the *Cornovii* (present day Flintshire and Denbighshire) which was concentrated mainly around hill forts (a line of them stretched along the length of the Clwydian Range in the eastern part of their territory). Their principal tribal centre was believed to be at Canovium. The historical texts say that Scapula *'ravaged the territory and collected extensive quantities of booty'* though it is believed that some action did take place the tribes stayed mainly in their hill forts and did not appear to cause any more problems for the Romans or their neighbours (there are records of the Deceangli trading lead and copper from their mines with the Romans, so there may have been some form of treaty agreed). Scapula's efforts at completing his campaign were cut short by an outbreak of violence amongst the *Brigantes* which required him to send forces to assist Queen Cartimanudua and so leaving the 'escape corridor' open.

The *Brigantes* tribe to the north of Plautius' frontier was a tribal confederacy (the largest in Britannia) and even though Queen Cartimandua had signed a treaty with the Romans, she did not have control over all of them; the *Brigantes* lands stretched from the west coast (Lancashire) and the east coast (Yorkshire) and its southern borders were adjacent to those of the *Cornovii* and the *Corieltavi.*

It is at this point Scapula decided that in order to better deal with the situation, he would move the XX Legion from Camulodunum to Glevum and construct a legion fort

(18.6 ha in size) as a forward base to attack the Silures. However, by removing the bulk of his current reserve force (XX Legion) to Glevum he had to ensure that he had a standing force still available to respond to any further incidents of rebellion. To do this he gained permission (presumably from Rome) to found a colonia at Camulodunum - it was named COLONIA VICTRICENSIS (the first of what would become the tribal civitates). This then, gave him the power to grant newly discharged legionaries land in exchange for them forming a military unit (while they were still fit and able) who would act as a fighting/police force if required. Yet another act fuelling the fires of resentment.

'Romanisation' of the annexed states and client kingdoms (those that had signed a treaty with Rome) was increasing and not necessarily to the benefit of the Britons. Rome's record when it came to dealing with these kingdoms was poor. Clearly tribal lands that had for generations belonged to the Trinovantes (around Camulodunum) were being arbitrarily confiscated and divided up among the army veterans.

Tacitus commented on the absolute indifference to the native ownership of land and Romans taking it for themselves as 'new settlers' and stated that *'the Trinovantes felt a bitter hatred for the veterans since these new colonists at Camulodunum had driven them out of their homes and off their land, calling them 'prisoners and slaves'. There was no help from the Roman soldiers as they encouraged the veteran's behaviour, as it would give them licence to do the same when they left the army'.*

It was not only the tribes people that were subject to Roman 'thievery'. The tribal leaders were 'invited' to join provincial councils, amongst whose duties were to oversee the 'Romanisation' of their lands and meet the costs themselves for new building projects as a way of 'accepting' Roman rule to such a point where they saw their wealth disappear into stone buildings. Faced with growing debts these leaders found no shortage of Romans willing to offer them loans to fulfill the works. A LOAN was a concept that these leaders did not truly understand and certainly had no understanding of interest added to the repayments. There was also the provincial 'taxation' implemented by the Procurator. For the local people the most onerous of which was the CORN REQUISITION used to feed the local Roman forts, it was also easy way for the Roman merchants to get their hands on grain. The tribes people were expected to deliver the food supplies at their own expense even if the fort was many miles away! Failure to do so would invite punitive measures. The valuable metal mines were now in the hands of Roman mining agents who could improve production at a cost to the local communities as they would reap little reward for their resources.

The kingdoms had signed the treaties with Rome on the condition that if they offered no resistance to Rome, Rome would help them... unfortunately it was becoming more obvious that this was not the case, disaffection was growing and swelling the armies of the resistance. None of this appears to have been of any consequence to Governor Scapula as he was intent on dealing with the 'Welsh' problem.

Note: Here again there is no mention, in any writings of this period of the Druid's interceding on behalf of the tribal leaders or inciting the people to the injustices being perpetrated by Roman officials.

Everything was now set to deal with the mountain dwelling tribes of the west... the Silures and the Ordovices.

Into the Land of the Resistance

Much of the land of the *Silures* was high barren plateau, poorly drained and boggy... the Black Mountains and the Brecon Beacons. The slopes of the hills and the valley floors were densely wooded; in approaching it the Romans first had to travel through the dense Forest of Dean. It is surmised (by Sheppard Frere) that the strength of the tribe, based on where the settlements were situated, lay on the coastal plains or in the valleys of the rivers Wye and Usk. It is relatively certain that they were a largely pastoral society, their territory containing multiple enclosures thought to be designed for herding, though crops would also have been planted.

To the west of this tribe (in Pembrokeshire and Carmarthenshire) were the *Demetae*, whose land was lower and more fertile, and possibly exposed to *Silures* raids. There are no records of any forts in this area pre or post Roman, implying that they were not an aggressive tribe and more likely to be pro-Roman.

To the north of these two tribes lay the land of the *Ordovices*, described in a little detail previously. It incorporated the Cambrian Mountains, much of central Wales and Snowdonia reaching up to the Menai Strait. They too, will have been a predominantly pastoral society, primarily herding with some agriculture, but a number of pre-Roman hill forts are in evidence here, suggesting that raiding did occur. It is possible that here also, there was a 'confederacy' of tribes rather than a single people. One thing is certain though, neither the *Silures* nor the *Ordovices* were prepared to accept the authority of Rome and all that went with it. Which is why it was here that Caratacus found tribes who would become a guerilla army he could lead, alongside others who had escaped from previous battles with the Romans, it proved to be a very effective force against the Roman troops and their allies.

The XX Legion had just been brought to Glevum in preparation for the campaign against the *Silures* when in AD 50, Caratacus launched an attack from his base somewhere in Glamorgan, deep into the lands of the *Dobunnii* (now a Roman client kingdom). He had already challenged Scapula in AD 47 whilst he was conquering the *Cornovii* but had been beaten back, so he moved his guerilla operations into the lands of the *Ordovices*. Scapula, along with the XX Legion, went after him. In order for Rome to rule, it had to defeat its opposition in open battle and neutralise any further threat; but guerilla warfare was going to make things difficult, especially with such an effective leader as Caratacus.

Ostorius Scapula and his troops did eventually catch up to the them; the tribesmen had halted at a hill fort that Caratacus had selected (*legend says Caer Caradog* [*Shropshire*], *but Llanymynech* [*Powys*] *better fits Tacitus' description*) to fight a decisive battle. He had chosen a site where he believed it was easy for the tribesmen to move forward and attack the Romans, and the advantage of an easy retreat if things did not go well for them in the battle. He also had to make it difficult for the Romans to attack his positions and a site that would be vulnerable for the Romans if it was they who had retreat. On the more gentle slopes the tribesmen had piled up stones to make a rampart. These warriors positioned themselves in front of these defences but they were still protected by a river which was in front of them. Tacitus describes the situation as *'Caratacus dashed about in all directions, telling his men that in the battle to come that day they would either begin to regain their freedom or be doomed to everlasting slavery. He recited the names of their ancestors, who had thrown out the tyrant Julius Caesar. Their bravery had kept them free from military oppression and reparations, and their wives and children safe from physical threat. The crowd responded to these and similar words with acclaim. Each soldier swore a solemn oath not to yield in the face of weapons or wounds.'* They believed that they had the upper hand on their chosen battleground whilst having the Roman troops 'hemmed' in by steep slopes.

Note: Here again there is no reference anywhere to the Druid's being present at this place, or of them shouting 'prayers to the heavens and curses upon the Romans'

As for Scapula, he was faced with a daunting sight of a river either side of which were stone ramparts and a hill fort filled with tribesmen. He surveyed the area and worked out the easiest way to attack and led his men, crossing the river without difficulty. When they reached the defences the British threw their missiles and the Romans suffered the worst casualties. It is quite probable that the Romans formed the 'testudo' with their shields from under which protection they would have torn down the loose stone ramparts and broken through. It would then have become a hand-to-hand fight, with the tribesmen able to retreat to higher ground. But this tactic ground was not enough to protect the tribesmen from the soldiers who followed up their attack. The lightly armed Roman soldiers harassed the enemy with missiles, while the heavily-armed soldiers closed in on them. They had no defence against Roman steel as they had no breast-plates or helmets to protect them and so they were cut down by the swords and javelins of the legionaries; if they turned around, they faced the spatha and spears of the auxiliaries. It was a great victory for the Romans and during the action they captured the wife and daughter of Caratacus, along with his brothers who had surrendered.

Following this defeat what remained of the tribal army fled further into Wales to continue a guerilla war against the Romans. Caratacus escaped into the land of the *Ordovices* through the 'Cheshire Gap' (*left open by Scapula when subduing the Deceangli*) and on to the Brigantes and Queen Cartimandua for protection (little knowing that she was already siding with the Romans to keep her kingdom). She duly handed him over (and would be well rewarded for it) to a jubilant Governor Scapula who in turn, sent Caratacus who had been fighting a successful guerilla war against the Romans for nearly 8 years to Rome with his family as a prize for Emperor Claudius. Yet, when this Celtic warrior spoke before the Emperor and the Senate, Claudius was so impressed by him that he allowed Caratacus and his family to live and remain in Rome for the rest of their days.

Caratacus had proved himself to be as a fearless warrior who had established himself as guerilla leader of the Welsh tribes (*Silures, Ordovician sand possibly some of the Deceangli*) An excellent leader of men, he carried out well-timed guerilla attacks deep into Roman 'territory'. He trained and instilled those tactics into the warriors of the *Silures* and *Ordovices*... which they would use to carry on the fight for many years to come. He was the most successful leader of the resistance against the Romans in Britannia and would live long in the memories of the Welsh tribes. So much so, that he was woven into the stories (the Celtic way of passing on heroic events through the generations) that would eventually find their way into the written word centuries later in the Mabinogion and folk tales of Snowdonia later under his Welsh name CARADOC.

Note: There are no records of Caratacus ever going to, being based on Mona or using it as a base for attacking Roman forces, forts, bases or towns.

Governor Publius Ostorius Scapula was so fuelled by his success of capturing Caratacus that he now turned his anger to finally defeating the *Silures* and *Ordovices* and publically vowed to annihilate them as *'the Romans had done to the Sugambri of Gaul and blotted them out of existence'*. This public declaration inflamed the tribes and they increased their attacks on the Roman patrols and foraging parties. On one raid by the *Silures*, a foraging party would have been totally massacred had Scapula himself not called out the Legion to defend the harried men. It was not only the declaration that had triggered this reaction; the Roman Auxiliary commanders had allowed their men to plunder indiscriminately, taking captives, seizing booty and behaving in an 'arrogant and high-handed' manner. However, even with this success, the all out war against these tribes in this west and mountainous region took its toll on Scapula, and he died of sickness in the winter of AD 51-52.

A new governor, Aulus Didius Gallus, was hastily sent by Emperor Claudius to take over only to find that the XX Legion (under Manlius Valens) had been defeated while in action against the *Silures* and *Ordovices*, but (according to Tacitus *Annals* 12.40) it was not as bad as the victors had made out. He had the legion return to the fort at Glevum (Gloucester) where combined forces of the XX and XIIII went on and annexed the lands of the *Demetae* (though it is likely that they were pro-Roman anyway, as no Roman forts were built in their region) which would give the Romans access to the gold mines at Dolaucothi (near present day Pumsaint)

Rather than continue these aggressive actions against

the tribes he set about stabilizing the border with new roads and forts, extending some into the 'borderlands' and establishing a larger fort at Viroconium. It may well have been at Emperor Claudius' instructions who may not have considered the benefits of further conquest in difficult terrain to be great enough to warrant the risk.

During his period of tenure as Governor, Emperor Claudius was murdered in Rome in AD 54 and Claudius' stepson Nero took over as Emperor. It was also during this period that the construction of a massive temple in Camulodunum (the seat of the Roman Governor) was completed. It included a 'Triumphal Arch' which proudly proclaimed Rome's domination, but to the Briton's it was seen as a reminder of their defeat, especially with the skewered heads of those who opposed Rome's occupation were put on display there. Winning over the 'hearts and minds' of the local populous was obviously not on the agenda.

Nero knew that vast sums of money being 'loaned' to the Britons under Claudius and now decided, because he was short of money (due to his largess for spending vast sums of money) to deal with it. As a first step he sent his tutor and adviser Seneca to Britannia and begin calling in the loans, fuelling anti-Roman feelings in the south-eastern part of the province.

Didius was then faced with unrest amongst the Brigantes (a consequence of Queen Cartimandua handing Caratacus, in manacles, over to the Romans.... the consequence of which would come back to visit her later when her kingdom split apart). Venutius and his faction were in dispute and fighting with his wife Cartimandua and her followers. She pleaded for help from Didius who responded by sending auxiliary troops to her aid and resolved the situation. He seems to have taken little military action anywhere after this.

Nero was in need of money for his projects in Rome and dealing with uprisings elsewhere. So he decided that further action was needed and Britannia was to be the answer. The action was to be on two levels. Firstly deal the *Silures* and the resistance in Wales (reducing his war chest costs). The second was to institute a civitates system in Britannia The civitates would be regional market towns complete, with a basilica and forum complex, providing an administrative and economic focus for the local region (it would also ban the tribes in using hill forts - except those being made into the civitates). Their primary purpose was to stimulate the local economy in order to raise taxes. All this activity was to be administered by an *ordo* or *curia*, a civitas council consisting of men of sufficient social rank to be able to stand for public office, a way of placing Roman officials in charge and reducing the power of the client kings. Nero did not like the idea of ' client kingdoms' as they were not under the direct rule of Rome, the civiates gave him that control.

In AD 57, Didius was removed and Nero appointed Quintas Veranius (a distinguished General and who had written a well received book on military tactics) to lead the conquest of Wales. Arriving in the winter of that year he set about the establishment of a legionary fortress at Viroconium, which would be the new base for the XIIII Legion drawing them back together from their vexillation forts around Shropshire (Manduessedum, Metchley and Leighton). Veranius campaigned with the XX Legion against the *Silures* in south Wales and did have some significant success including establishing a new fort on the river Usk. He also had troops of the VIIII Legion now based at forts in Newton-on-Trent, Longthorpe and Great Casterton to keep a watch on the Brigantes for any further signs of trouble. The II Legion was busy subduing the tribes in Devon and

Cornwall. However it was to be a short campaign for Veranius, he died within a year still believing that he would have completed his mission within two years.

During this time, the second phase of Nero's wishes was being put into action; he appointed a new *procurator*, Decianus Catus, (the official responsible for provincial expenditure and collection of taxes – directly responsible to the Emperor) to call in the loans, on behalf of Nero, that had been made to tribal leaders under Emperor Claudius (those who had agreed to offer no resistance to Rome and whom Rome had promised to help), and also to begin the creation of the *civitates* (which included the policy of preventing the tribes from using or fortifying their hill forts). Two key points of Roman Imperial domination in conquered states would now be put into action:-

- Drawing the tribes people into urban centres required their 'civilizing' to keep them under control.
- By feeding these urban centres, people were free to work to make goods; goods equals taxes and wealth, and wealth equals power.

This process then creates a wealth and power identity for the individual and the tribal identity becomes less important making the population easier to control via the purse rather than the heart.

AD 58 and Emperor Nero appoints Gaius Seutonius Paulinus Governor of Britannia, who would play a key part in what was to befall Mona and the Druids.

Governor Gaius Seutonius Paulinus: AD 58 - 61

Statue representing Seutonius Paulinus at the Roman Baths in Aquae Sulis.

Little is known of Seutonius Paulinus before AD 40 but he was believed to have been serving as a praetor (a magistrate for the administration of justice), but where is not known.

In AD 40 he was appointed governor of Mauretania (the region of we know today as Morocco, western Algeria and the Atlas Mountains). In collaboration with Gnaeus Hosidius Geta (the commander of the Legio VIIII Hispania) he suppressed a revolt in this mountainous province (he was the first Roman General to cross the Atlas Mountains in this campaign), which had arisen from the execution of its Moor ruler - ordered by Emperor Caligula in 41 AD (Cassius Dio . *Roman History* 60.9).

In 58 AD, after having presumably served as a Roman Consul *(possibly of Mauretania)* for a period of time, he was appointed governor of Britannia. His proven success in fighting in the mountains of Mauretania may have been the reason that Emperor Nero decided to have Paulinus take on the mountain tribes in 'Wales' and finally have the majority of Britannia under Roman rule; the resistance had been going on for too long and had to be dealt with.

Tacitus said of Paulinus *'he was driven by ambition to emulate the recent glorious successes in Armenia of his colleague*

Gnaeus Domitius Corbulo... rival both in military expertise and reputation among the people which lets no-one go unchallenged. His ambition was to defeat the enemy and so equal Corbolo's glory'.

He arrived to find that Roman domination was still basically south of the line between the Wash and the Severn, whereas to the north of this line the situation was more unstable. The last 3 governors had been unable to solve the problem of the continued raids on Roman troops and their 'allies' by the *Silures* and the *Ordovices*. It appears that he believed his mission was to break these tribes and destroy the Druids.

It is clear from the Roman historian writings, that apart from the ongoing military activity, the 'Romanisation' of the annexed and client kingdoms in southern Britannia was increasing but not necessarily to the benefit of the Britons, in fact it is was getting worse.

This new governor took over a regime that had the Roman military in charge of mining all mineral reserves in the Weald (Iron) and Gloucestershire (Lead and Silver in the Mendips). Tribal lands were being arbitrarily confiscated and divided up between veterans of the Roman army creating bitter hatred amongst the tribesmen of these new 'settlers'. No justice was forthcoming from the Roman military (or the praetor – the Roman magistrate responsible for the administration of justice) as they had encouraged the veterans behaviour, as it would give them licence to do so when they left the army.

The 'draining' of the tribal kings wealth was also continuing as their oppidia (large fortified iron age settlements in their tribal lands) were being converted into civitates as Emperor Nero had instructed; Calleva Atrebatum, Camulodunum, Venta Belgarum, Ratae Corieltauvarum, Verulamium and Novimagus Reginorum. The procurator,

Decianus Catus, was following his Emperors orders 'You know my needs and let's make sure that no one is left with anything'. The Roman's treatment on the tribes was reaching the point of arrogant disdain. Catus's actions after the death of Boudicca's husband, Prasatugas, would be the spark that nearly lost Rome Britannia.

For the next two years Governor Paulinus continued the work of his predecessor, with some success, of aggressively subduing the tribes on the western border. The Roman road, Watling Street, now reached Viroconium so that supplies, materials and men could move quickly up from the south. He also strengthened the garrisons and completed (and increased) the number of forts in this region:

Viroconium	Legionary fortress for Legio XIIII
Glevum	Vexillation fortress for Legio XX
Burrium (on the Usk)	Vexillation fortress for Legio XX
Aquae Sulis	Fort for cohors of Legio XX and Ala I Thracum

It is quite possible that during this period he was making preparations in the planning of the campaign against the *Ordovices*, the Druids and Mona. The establishment of these above forts may have been part of the planning. To that end, he must have been receiving information reports about the activities and strength of the resistance forces in the mountain homesteads of the *Ordovices*, the Strait that separated the mainland from the island and the forces that he would be up against on Mona itself. Tacitus, Annals 14.29 states '*...the island of Mona which had a powerful population and was refuge for fugitives*'. No mention of Druids at all, clearly they were no military threat.

There are no classical text references to what military and logistical forces Paulinus brought together for this campaign. The only reference to the forces he had under his direct command during this time was when he had to quickly abandon Mona and deal with the Boudican revolt in the south which was escalating rapidly.

Tacitus states in Annals 14.34 that *'Paulinus marched with the XIIII Legion, veterans of the XX Legion and auxiliaries from the neighbourhood, in total numbering* 10,000 *men'*

It is credible to surmise that as Paulinus marched back towards the advancing rebels, with some indication of the size of force he was going to have to deal with, also with the knowledge of the death and destruction that had already befallen the south east, he would have pulled in as many auxiliary forces on route as possible for the coming battle. If this is the case, then it is likely that the attacking force going to Mona would have been based around the XIIII Legion, (as this was best placed being based at Viroconium, close to the border with the eastern *Ordovices* lands) and possibly a vexillation of the XX Legion.

The Romans were well aware of the difficulties of moving Legions and equipment through mountains and forests (Paulinus did have experience of this in the Atlas Mountains with Roman troops, and in the forest of Germania with the XIIII and XX Legion). He would also be mindful of what occurred in AD 9 when 3 Roman Legions were defeated by Arminius and the German tribes in the Teutoburg Forest (with the loss of all 3 Legion Aquila – their golden eagle Standards) when planning his strategy. As for the XIIII Legion, before being brought to the invasion of Britannia they had been based in Moguntiacum (Mainz) on the river Rhine and had crossed it - *information which bares relevance later* - to fight against Arminius, leader of the Germanic tribes.

There is also the distinct possibility that he also took Batavian auxiliaries (and Thracian cavalry), as they would be useful in the crossing of the Menai Strait in the initial attack force (they have proved their worth and skills in tactics when they secretely crossed the rivers Medway and Thames and helping to rout the Catavellauni forces and their allies early in the invasion of Britannia).

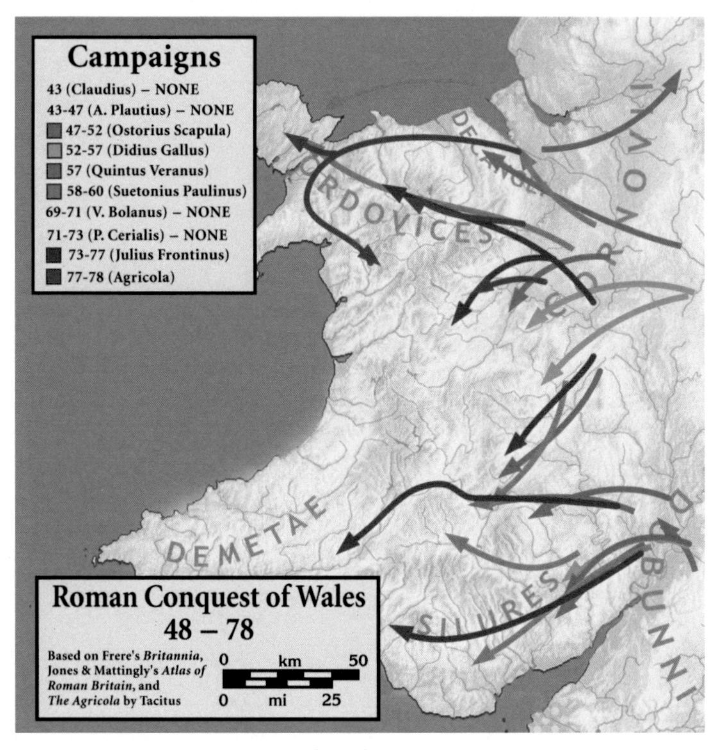

Roman Conquest of Wales. (Wikimedia Commons)

Prior to Paulinus' attack on the Ordovician lands there had only been limited military incursions into western Britannia. It would be the consequences of the actions taken by the previous Governors and Paulinus against the inhabitants of Britannia they already ruled that would mean that it would bee over a decade military action was taken again in the west.

The Ordovices

In order for the Romans to make a land attack from the shoreline opposite Mona, they would first have to pass through the valleys of the mountainous region of the Ordovices tribe.

The approximate distribution of native pre-Roman settlements in Wales.

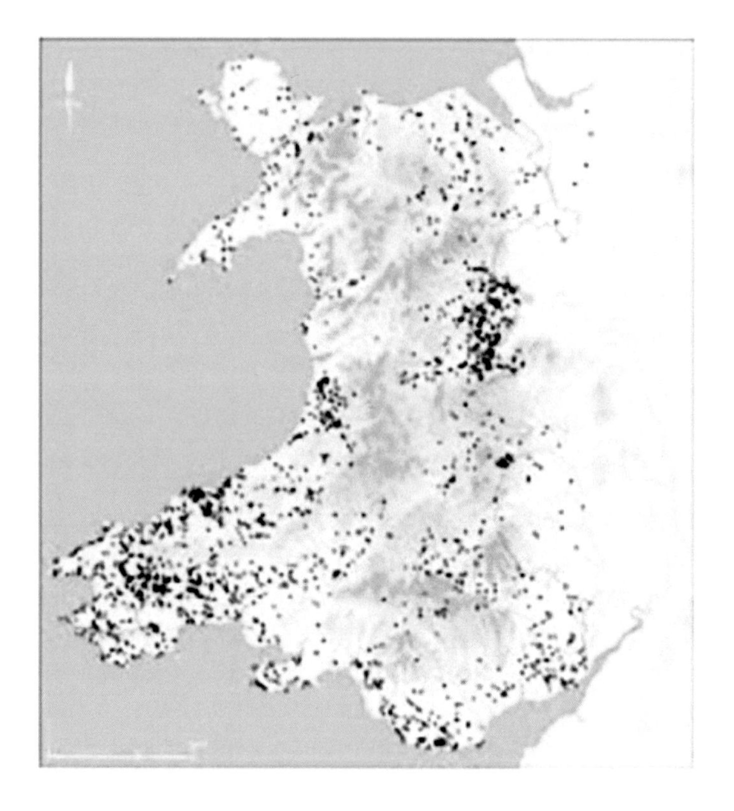

Image: Courtesy of the Gwynedd Archaeological Trust

There are almost 600 known hill forts in Wales
(J Davies,1993)

It is difficult to know how the inhabitants of this region of western Britannia saw or defined themselves. There is little evidence during this period of any large tribal communities, more a scattered population of tribal 'families' in a long established Celtic culture but who appear to have spoken a variation of a shared celtic language. Edward Lhuyd (1660-1709), a linguist, published the *Archaeologies Britannica, Histories and Customs of Great Britain* in 1707 after travelling and studying the languages of Wales, Cornwall, Bas-Bretagne, Ireland and Scotland. In his first volume he recorded that he had found similarities between 2 families of the Celtic language: the Brythonic or P- Celtic (no q in the alphabet) spoken by the Bretons, Cornish and Welsh - which he believed had originated in Gaul. The 2nd was Q – Celtic, Gaelic, (no p in the alphabet) spoken in Ireland, Isle of Man and Scotland. They would have been able to communicate but with some differences, similar to todays population where dialects can cause minor problems even though the language is still English. The *Ordovician* tribe (as designated by Ptolomy) of which we have no recorded physical description, is believed to have mainly inhabited south Gwynedd and south Clwyd including parts of what we now know as western Shropshire and Hereford & Worcester. From current archaeological evidence they did not appear to have had an oppidia, a trading centre for their culture but rather appear to have lived in small independent homesteads called *Tre* (more than one house together would be *Tref/i*). It should be added that there is a suggestion that Caerhun in the Conwy Valley and Branogenium, may have served in part as a tribal capital of sorts or as a defensible market place (the latter site was made up of several camps and forts). There is clear evidence that the land they are reputed to have occupied is littered with hill forts of all different sizes but very few large ones (*ref above*) suggesting that the people may well have lived in the immediate environs of the forts and used them only when they were threatened by raiders. Several hill forts can be attributed to the eastern half of the Ordovician territory; Castell Dinas Bran, Moel y Gaer (today known as Llantisilio), Caer Drwyn and Caer Euni, all in the Deva valley within easy striking distance of the lowland territories of the Cornovii in the region of Caer Ogyrfan (Oswestry).

On the other (southern) side of the Berwyn range from these settlements, there is a hill fort at Craig Rhiwarth deep in the Tanat valley at the extreme northern tip of Powys. This fort appears to mark the boundary between the *Ordovices* and their neighbours the *Cornovii*.

The western part of their tribal territory included Dinas Emrys at the foot of Cadair Berwyn, Moel Goedog overlooking the mouth of the Tisobis Fluvius (one of the few welsh rivers recorded by the Romans) near Harlech, and a number of forts along the length of the Ganganorum Prom, from Dinas Dinlle on the north coast, overlooking the southern Menai and Mona, to Castell Odo on the south-western tip. Another possible fort was at Dinas Dinorwig overlooking the Menai Strait.

What is not clear is how they lived as archaeological finds can only give us a snap shot of their lives. Most of the remains of the settlements seen today are variations of the roundhouse with grave goods providing the main source of information in respect of day to day life and what was valuable to them. Much of the land they occupied was mountainous and would probably have only been good enough for sheep and cattle herding. The valleys would have served as arable farming but not on the scale seen in the

Dinas Dinlle

lowlands to the east (the tribal occupation sites appear to be relatively small). Certainly there were warriors within this tribe, their presence alongside Caratácus, raiding into *Cornovii* territory and at the battle of Caer Caradog gives us that evidence, but we know little else about them as fighters.

The fact that Caratacus employed hit and run tactics against the Romans and their allies suggests that full scale battles were not their way of fighting, unlike the set short battle tactics used by the lowland Britannic and European tribes. It begs the question as to their stamina and endurance in a long battle when it came, compared to that of the battle-hardened Roman soldier.

Personal Weapons

Swords

The Britannic tribes are recorded as having used the shorter iron sword rather than their European counterparts. They were similar in length to the Roman gladius. It is not known whether all had swords. Females were also allowed to fight as they were equal to men in much of the Celtic culture, and are known to have been present on the fighting line on the Menai Strait opposite Paulinus' troops; clear from Tacitus's description.

Shields – **Caetra style**

The examples of shields found in burial mounds or in lakes and ponds (votive offerings) for this time period are usually round or an elongated oval shape, between 30 and 90 cm in diameter. On the front was usually a hollow wood shield boss (covered in metal) both to protect the hand and to be used to 'punch' against their enemy. On the inside of the boss hole was a handle to hold the shield. The shields were made of wood, usually oak or lime wood. Generally covered with leather (plain wooden shields could easily break and shatter after a number ofdirect blows Roman Scorpio bolts or disabled with a hit from a pilum). They decorated with a variety of celtic designs but not in the same fashion as the standard design on the scutum of the Roman army.

Spears

Again, evidence found in burial mounds that indicates spears were part of the warrior's weapons. From the size of narrow leaf-shaped spear heads it has been estimated the spear would have been up to 2 metres in length. Both spears and javelins were known to have been in the Britannia tribes arsenal

Slingshots

Piles of small rounded stones found at Caer Caradoc (Shropshire) would have been used in these simple weapons. It was known to have been the dominant missle weapon in Britannia at this time, so it is more than likely to have been part of the *Ordivician* artillery and an extremely effective weapon in the right hands.

As to the use of bows and arrows, there is currently little evidence to show that they were used in battle, more for hunting.

The horse drawn war chariots used in large numbers were favoured by the Britannic tribes, but to date there is no evidence to suggest that they were present on Mona or indeed the mainland of the *Ordovices*. The topography of the land in this region would have limited its use and therfore its value in any aggressive action.

Helmets and Body Armour

There are records of the tribal warriors having bronze helmets with ornate patterns but no mention of any armour. It is fair to summarise therefore that it would not have been available to the common man and they would have fought in tunics and cloaks.

From descriptions of battles with the Romans, the Britannic warriors style was more about making themselves, as individuals, looking as fierce as possible (using woad, lime wash in their hair and in fact there are accounts of some celtic warriors fighting naked) rather than be organised into orderly battle lines. Their attacks were a series of charges at the enemy, fall back and charge again, as continuous battle was not their style of fighting. Apart form those men of the tribe who were warriors (the knights and their trained men) most would have been men drawn in from the homesteads to fight who would have had little or no experience of fighting.

Defence

A great number of the settlements in the Ordovician lands had some form of defensive hill fort. They were primarily built of stone blocks piled on top on one another; techniques/compounds for binding the stones together to make a more substantial barrier appear to not have been used at that time. Many of these hill forts were only occupied in time of threat from raiders etc so would have been only a temporary defence until the threat was over. Few have been found with any source of water e.g a well (again confirming that these were temporary sites) not ideal if you are surrounded by Roman troops.

When the Roman troops came up against them they would form a testudo (the tortoise) position, their shields interlocked over their heads and flanks for protection whilst troops underneath were able to drag stones out of the walls and eventually break through without too much difficulty. This actually did occur at the Battle of Caer Caradoc where the Romans broke through the *Ordovician* defensive ramparts that Caratacus had thought had been a good defensible position.

Training and Skills

The basic unit of 'celtic' life was the clan, a sort of extended family (estimated in the Ordovician territory as being up to to 100 individuals, based on the number of dwellings/homesteads) who were all responsible for each other. These clans were bound together into a 'confederation style' tribe for protection, structure and trading. Here there has to be a certain number of assumptions made, because there are no records of how they met the Romans in battle. The social structure of many of the tribes in Britannia functioned in a similar pattern. Firstly there was the Cheiftain or King, then a band of warriors (nobles) who could be considered as regular soldiers (used for defence or raiding parties). The main populace (both men and women fought in this celtic society) would have been called to arms in an emergency. How much training these individuals received is speculative, most of their time would have been spent herding their livestock and well possible working the land. So it is more than likely that they would have been just numbers on the battlefield. Also there is little archaeological evidence of chariots in this part of Britannia, the terrain may well have been a deciding factor in their absence.

It is certainly possible that during the time when Caratacus was leading the Ordovician warriors against the Romans, much of remainder of the populace further to the north and west never engaged in any warfare with Roman troops but continued with their everyday lives. After the defeat at Caer Caradoc and the incusions of Roman troops into the eastern zone of their lands and the influx of refugees who would have been coming along the trails westward fleeing the Roman 'tyranny' there may well have been more involvement from the homsteads as tribal warriors lost in the battle and skirmishes would have needed to be replaced.

There was no question as to their prowess for war, but their style of war was to challenge their opponents fighting as individuals not as units, charging their enemies on mass; shouting curses and oaths at the top of their voices (as described in Tacitus' account on the Menai Strait) attack, fall back and attack again. It was not the continuous battle style that the Romans used, the tribesmen would not have had the stamina (or indeed training) for a consistent long battle, which proved to be a serious weakness in their resistance against the Romans fighting against them (most of the classical accounts of the battles between the Britannia tribes and the Romans between 43 AD and 80 AD seem to confirm this). It can also be backed up when looking at how Caratacus led and trained the *Ordovices* warriors; they fought hit and run tactics with the Romans and their allies. It is fairly safe to say that he fully understood that they would fail to win full scale battles (from his experience at the battles of the Medway and Thames) against these Roman Legions, this was not their way of fighting and they would lose. The short sharp encounters were therfore more suited to their fighting style and that it would wear the Romans down. He had recognised that the tribesmen stamina for a long battle when it came, would fail them, unlike the Roman soldier who was trained to hold his position and fight all day with the support of his cohort comrades.

Yet this formidable Roman army could be beaten. Ambushing a column of soldiers in an area where these Romans could not deploy their defensive and attacking formations made them just as vulnerable as the ill trained forces they had attacked throughout the empire.

This was graphically shown in the Teutoburg Forest where 3 legions, 6 cohorts of auxiliaries and cavalry plus families their entourage and camp followers were killed in an ambush by Germanic tribesmen. They had chosen to set a trap at a point where the Roman column would have been stretched out into a narrow line (probably a 15 kilometres or more in length) because of the terrain (steep cliffs on one side and marsh on the other) which prevented the Romans from deploying defensive formations. The tribesmen having attacked and killed the head of the column could then attack the rest at will as the rest of the column would not have been aware of the attack so far ahead of them.

What was required was a leader who could hold his men to order and find the right place to ambush.

Note: The tribes of Wales: *Ordovices, Gangani, Deceangli, Silures and Demetea*, would most likely have belonged to the Brythonic branch of the 'Celtic' language along with the tribes of Corwall, Cumbria and the Bretons of northern France.

The Druids (*Welsh – Derwydd*)

It is not the author's intention to go into the origins of the Druids, as this has been covered by eminent historians already, but to try and understand how their teachings and position were so emeshed within the Britannic tribes. Why was Mona so important to them and ultimately, what was the reason that the Roman Governor felt it necessary to send a large force to the island in order to wipe them out and presumably break their 'power' within the Britannic tribes.

The Druidic system was a tripartite order, the number 3 was important in their belief system. Their 3 precepts were; worship the gods, be manly and tell the truth.

Strabo, Geographica IV, 4,C, 197

'Among all the Gallic peoples, generally speaking, there are 3 categories of men who are held in exceptional honour: Bards (Bardi), Vates (Ouvates/Euhages) and Druids. The Bards are singers and poets, the Vates are diviners, astrologers and natural philosophers. The Druids, in addition to natural philosophy also study moral philosophy and medicines. They are considered the most just of men and on this account they are entrusted with the decision not only of the private disputes, but of public disputes as well. So that in former times they even arbitrated in cases of war and made opponents stop when they were about to line up for battle'

Ammianus Macellinus XV,9.4.

'It was the custom of the Bards to celebrate the brave deeds of their famous men in epic verse accompanied by the gentle strains of the lyre. The Euhages (Vates) stove to explainthe high mysteries of nature [natural philosophy]. Then came the Druids,

men of greater talent. They were uplifted by searchings into the secret and sublime things [natural and moral philosophy] and professed the immortality of the soul and divination'.

Similar classical accounts are recorded by Cicero (*De Divinatione, I,xli. 9*), Diodorus Siculus (*Histories.V,28,6*), Seutonius (*The Twelve Ceasars, Claudius, 25*), Pomponius Mela (*De Situ Orbis, III, 2, 18 and 19*), and Pliny (*Natural Histories, XVI, 249*).

There are a few historical accounts dating from the 17th and 18th Centuries during whichthere was seemingly a sudden interest in the Druids. This suggest that there were in fact more categories of this social caste, but the general consensus based on texts from the 2nd Century onwards appear to agree on the tripartite structure. There are clear observations that these Druids were learned in the arts of medicines, religious rites and astronomy (which keyed in to their religious rites). The Druids were reputed to have computed time by night, not days; a custom which they had handed down from their remote ancestors and which they confirmed by their measuring of time by the moon. They had calculated the year as a lunar cycle of 12 and the season within that. As Pliny records *'They began both their months and years, not from the change, but from the sixth day of the moon'*. The changes of the moon cycle were used by them to engage in specific sacred and civil rights; which is probably why the collection of the mistletoe on the sixth day was so auspicious to them. He also states that Druidism had its origins in Gaul and was transplanted into Brittania (xxi.1). The Gauls and the tribes of Britannia were superstitious peoples, and would have held the Druids in high regard because of their wisdom and learning and would have made much use of the advice given by them. From what texts there are, it is evident that due to their knowledge of herbs and medicines the tribal leaders also went on to expect them to care for their health: the Celts probably saw a clear connection between the arts of healing and religion.

The Druid 'religion' was banned in Rome. According to Pliny the Elder, in his texts around AD 70, Emperor Tiberius (AD 14 – AD 37) introduced laws that banned not only Druidic practices but also other native soothsayers and healers who may have been involved in human/animal sacrifices. Yet another by Seutonius Tranquillius writing in 2nd century AD claimed that Rome's first emperor, Augustus (27 BC – AD 14) had decreed that no-one could be both a Druid and a Roman citizen, and later that Claudius (AD 41 – AD 54) in his 12 Lives of Caesar, Chapter 25 *'The religious rites of the Druids, solemnized by such cruelties, which have been forbidden the citizens of Rome during the reign of Augustus, he utterly abolished among the Gauls'*.

It therefore appears that this 'religion' had migrated eastwards from Gaul (probably via slaves brought in from captured territories) into Roman society itself, to a point where Rome felt the need to ban it completely. Yet this action does not seem to relate whatsoever to the reason for the events that would be take place in AD 60. The only information we have is from records of observations made in the 1st century's BC and AD which may give us some insight as to what could have changed their view of the Druids.

Julius Caesar, in his campaigns in Gaul and Celtica in 55 – 53 BC made a number of references to the Druids located there. Information he apparently gained from a member of the Druidic order called Diviciacus the Aeduan who was an admirer of Rome and a friend of Caesar's. He may as a matter of politic not exposed all parts of the Druid's actvities to an antagonist of his culture.

Caesar, Commetarii De Bello Gallico VI, 13

'The Druids are concerned with worship of the gods, look after public and private sacrifice and expound on religious matters. A large number of young men flock to them for training and hold them in high favour. They are said there to learn by heart a great number of verses; accordingly some remain in the course of training for twenty years. For they have the right to decide nearly all public and private disputes and they also pass judgement, decide rewards and penalties in criminal and murder cases as well as disputes concerning legacies and boundaries. This institution is supposed to have been devised in Britain, and to have been brought over from it into Gaul; and now those who desire to gain a more accurate knowledge of that system generally proceed thither for the purpose of studying it.'

Note: The first clear record that the Druid religion was active in Britannia.

Caesar, Commetarii De Bello Gallico VI, 14

'The Druids usually hold aloof from war, and do not pay war taxes with the rest; they are excused from military service and exempt from all liabilities. Tempted by these great rewards, many young men assemble of their own motion to receive their training; many are sent by parents and relatives. Report says that in the schools of the Druids they learn by heart a great number of verses, and therefore some persons remain twenty years under training. And they do not think it proper to commit these utterances to writing, although in almost all other matters, and in their public and private accounts, they make use of Greek letters. I believe that they have adopted the practice for two reasons — that they do not wish the rule to become common property, nor those who learn the rule to rely on writing and so neglect the cultivation of the memory; and, in fact, it does usually happen that the assistance of writing tends to relax the diligence

of the student and the action of the memory. The cardinal doctrine which they seek to teach is that souls do not die, but after death pass from one to another; and this belief, as the fear of death is thereby cast aside, they hold to be the greatest incentive to valour. Besides this, they have many discussions as touching the stars and their movement, the size of the universe and of the earth, the order of nature, the strength and the powers of the immortal gods, and hand down their lore to the young men'.

Henry Rowlands (1655-1723) the local Rector in Llanidan, Mona, in his work *'Mona Antiqua Restaurata: An Archaeological Discourse on the Antiquites Natural and Historical, of the Isle of Anglesey. The Ancient Seat of the British Druids'* discusses why the Druids actually chose Ynys Môn as their home and cultural training center. In it he postulates that there are 2 reasons why they chose the island (a point of view which has much insight and merit) ...

'the first is that its natural appearance and prospect might well enough endear them [Druid] *the choice of it for their feat and habitation. It was an island, and therefore, fittest of any place (as being more solitary and less incommoded with affrightments of war and tumult and is a pleasant island with springs and rivers, fruitful soil and bountiful seas'...'the second is a political consideration likewise of its site and position, we may well suppose, did no less oblige these men of thought and retirement... here again the advantage was twofold. First is that is was an island, defended by the sea on every side and therefore best fortified and secured against the alarms and incursions of prevailing aggressors that, at that time frequent inland countries ... and though divided from the continent (mainland Britannia) by an arm of the sea, able to safeguard them from all approaches of danger, yet they were near enough to it to receive friends or communicate with them any hour of the year. The second it was of a just proportion and latitude within itself, suitable to the ends*

intended, that is solitude and safety. It was not too big and of too large an extent, where it might nourish parties and factions which might endanger its repose and tranquillity. It was not too small and scarcity to enfeeble and starve itself, but was as I said of a bigness and proportion to support and maintain itself in plight and vigour, in safety and security from all accidents, and particularly fitted to have it's rule and government moulded to a monastic economy which these Druids were now introducing'.

Unlike the Romans and the Greek, the Druids did not have stone temples in which to worship, theirs was very much out in the open and closer to nature, the sacred oak groveswith its inner sanctum. Away from these sacred places the Druids would sit on mounts or hillocks that they called GORFEDDAÛ and 'pronounce their decrees and sentences and made their solemn orations to the people'.

There are quite a few classical references [by Siculus, Strabo, Pliny, Marcellinus, Mela and Chrysostom] to the rituals and teachings of the Druids, all with a similar tale to tell........ *'the Druids seemingly conducted their religious services in the open air, and their scared places were often close to water and oak trees (especially those bearing mistletoe*). Pliny the Elder in his *Natural History XVI, 95* recorded the Celtic religious ceremony of *'The Ritual of Oak and Mistletoe'* in which white-clad Druids climbed a sacred oak on the sixth day and cut down the mistletoe growing on it, sacrificed two white bulls and used the mistletoe to make an elixir to cure infertility and the effects of all poisons. They appear to have been well versed in the use of herbs and plants for curative purposes. There are other records of animals and humans being sacrificed during ceremonies either for divination or punishment; Caesar wrote about the Wicker Man, a giant wooden effigy within which criminals (and innocents?) were burnt alive to placate the gods.

The Celts of Gaul and Britannia are believed to have thought that internal diseases proceeded immediately from the anger of the Gods and the only ways of obtaining relief for that individual was to apply to their priests (the Druids) for religions rites and sacrifice. Caesar stated that *'They (Celts) are much addicted to superstitions and for this cause, those that are afflicted with dangerous diseases sacrifice a man, or promise that they will sacrifice one for their recovery'*. The Celts would have looked to the Druids for assistance in judicial matters, which is probably why there are a number of corroborating records regarding the sacrificial rites and punishments that they officiated at and which were not just about the act of justice against a criminal.

According to the Encyclopedia Britannica: Or Dictionary of Arts, Sciences and Miscellaneous Literature, 1823, Vol VI, pp 138-142...... *'the Druids worshipped the supreme being under the name of ESUS or HESUS and the symbol of the oak. They worshipped in the scared recess, in which no other person was allowed to enter unless they carried a chain in token of his absolute dependants on the deity'*.

An observation by Pliny does offer some clarity as to the way the Druids and the tribes people were so interwoven *'from the incantations and magical rites that are in evidence at the time* [from the Druids], *there was no doubt that magic derived its origin from medicine and that by its flattering but dilutive promises it came to be esteemed as the most sublime and sacred part of the art of healing'*. The various aspects of the Druids knowledge of all things around them, (nothing was committed to writing or inscription) truly set them apart from the tribesmen, who it seems saw them as their councillors, healers, educators, the hands of justice and priests. So much so, it is difficult to understand why there is so little mention of them in the Roman campaigns, and peace treaties with the Britannic tribes as Rome moves across the island.

Druidism seems to have been one of the many religions of this period. Diogenes Leartius assures us in his prologue *VITAE Book V* that *'the Druids were the same among the ancient Britons as the Magi of the Persians, the Chaldeans of Assyria and Babylonia, and the Gymnosophistae of the Indians'* and yet they were not treated as a threat to these empire builders. So who or what changed the 'face' of Druidism; was it that they spiralled into barbaric acts which appalled 'civilised' Roman society or was there a political motivation in changing the view of this religion.

An event which occurred during the Roman civil war, between Caesar on one side and the consul Pompey with the Roman Senate on the other, may well have been the turning point which cast the Druids in a different light although the events are not recorded in Caesar's writings. Marcus Annaeus Lucanus (AD 30 – 65) who gained much favour with Emperor Nero (for a while at least) described the event in his poem *PHARSALIA* (also known as de *Bello Civili*) and may have had some influence on their view point; depending of course on how the poem was presented to Nero and his followers. In 49 BC the Roman proconsul of Gaul (Lucius Ahenobarbus) was sent by the Roman Senate to gain control of the Greek controlled city of Massilia (the Massiliots had sided with Roman Senate and Pompey against Caesar) in order to prevent Caesar from going through it to Hispania and attacking Pompey's forces. Caesar laid siege to Massilia but could not break through. He looked for materials to build siege weapons including a stationary tower 30 ft. square and six stories in height against the very walls of the city to break the city's defences. At this point it is better to leave the description of what occurred next to Lucanus concerning the Druid Grove of

Andraste (devoted to either Andrasta – the Celtic mother goddess associated with war or Adrasteia – goddess of revolt, retribution and justice) near Massilia.

'A grove there was untouched by men's hands from ancient times, whose interlacing boughs enclosed a space of darkness and cold shade, and banished the sunlight from above. No rural pan dwelt no Silvanus ruler of the woods, no nymphs; but gods were worshipped there with savage rites, the altars were heaped with hideous offerings, and every tree was sprinkled with human gore. On those boughs birds feared to perch, in those covets wild beasts would not lie down; no wind ever bore down upon that wood, nor thunderbolt hurled from the black clouds, the trees even spread their leaves to no breeze rustled of themselves. Water also, fell there in abundance from dark springs. The images of the gods, grim and rude were uncouth blocks formed of felled tree trunks. Their mere antiquity and ghastly hue of their rotten timber struck terror; men feel less awe of deities worshipped under familiar forms; so much does it increase their sense of fear, not to know the gods whom they dread. Legend also told that often the subterranean hollows quaked and bellowed, that yew trees fell down and rose again, that the glare of the conflagration came from the trees that were not on fire and that serpents twined and glided round the stems. The people never resorted thither to worship at close quarters but left the place to the gods. For when the sun is in the mid-heaven or dark night fills the sky, the priest himself dreads their approach and fears to surprise the lord of the grove. This grove was sentenced by Caesar to fall before the strike of the axe; for it grew near his works. Spared in earlier warfare, it stood there covered with trees among hills already cleared. But strong areas faltered and the men awed by the solemnity and terror of the place, believed that if they aimed a blow at the sacred trunks, their axes would rebound against their own limbs. When Caesar saw that his soldiers were sore

hindered and paralysed, he was the first to snatch an axe and swing it, and dared to cleave a towering oak with the steel, driving the blade into the desecrated wood, he cried 'Believe that I am guilty of sacrilege and thenceforth none of you need fear to cut down the tree'. Then all men obeyed his bidding; they were not easy in their minds nor had their fears been removed; but they weighed Caesar's wrath against the wrath of heaven. Ash trees were felled, gnarled Holm-oaks overthrown, Dodonna's oak and alder that suits the sea., the cypress that bears witness to a monarch's grief, all lost their leaves for the first time, robbed of their foliage they let in the daylight and the toppling wood, when smitten, supported itself by the close growth of it's timber'.

In actual fact, Caesar was recorded as having left soon after this 'first cut of the tree' is supposed to have occurred, and had placed his trusted Legate, Gaius Trebonius in charge, with 3 legions to build the siege tower out of local stone and the wood to be hewn, to break through and take over Massilia.

Note: A Coincidence or retribution by the Celtic Gods for the desecration of the Grove?.......

Julius Caesar was assassinated in 44 BC.

Gaius Trebonius was among those who instigated the plot to assassinate Caesar. Unfortunately for Trebonius, he was captured a year after Caesar's death, tortured and beheaded.

The 3 Legions - XV11, XV111 and XIX were newly formed for this campaign. They would have been involved in the siege and probably the destruction of the Grove, were completely wiped out 58 years later in the Teutoberg Forest by a force of Germanic tribes.

From Lucanus' narrative it is clear that he was building up the fear and terror of the Grove, and what horrors that could have occured there. All the surrounding woodland had already gone and yet the local tribes had still left the Grove well alone. So was there some other motivation regarding the 'horror' of the grove?. Possibly to justify severe punitive actions at a later date against the Druids and their practices?

Or may be not... looking deeper into the information in the classical texts it is clear that when the Druids practices/rites were banned by the Roman Emperors in the Ist Century AD it was as Seutonius described it in Claudius 25.. *'this action was neither suppression or persecution but a declaration against elements of their practices which were out of bounds of the policy of Roman toleration'* That said, these acts are recorded as have been carried out in the presence of (but not including the actual act of blood letting or human sacrifice) the Druids/Druidesses who undertook the divination as a result of the acts. The records appear to only cover the region of the Gauls, there is little detail as to what was happening elsewhere where the Druids held sway. The Romans under their own gods also carried out sacrifices in order to gain insight into future events, but it appears they drew the line when it came to human sacrifice!! It may well be that these Groves of the Druids were used for certain sacrifices, but it is clear that in many more cases than not these 'sacrfices' were tribal judgements against offenders of their law. The Druids did or were asked to carry out divination as part of the practice and , which would not have been done in the sacred groves but in a public place. As for the Grove itself and the' gore etc 'covering the bark of the trees there may be another explanation (not known by or perhaps ignored by Roman authorities). Having researched trees that existed in this period (and still do today) there may be a more simple explanation. It is quite possible that their age and health may have exaggerated their appearance to the onlooker...

Oak trees, when they are in decline they can suffer from dark fluid oozing from cracks in their bark.
Horse Chestnut trees, suffer from 'Bleeding Canker'; a rusty red/yellow fluid oozing from the bark and which turns into a black gummy substance.

Both these trees were native to SE Europe at that time. It does beg the question how much was ''gore' and how much was the natural cycle of the trees? or was this the first ever use of political propaganda against a powerful cult? The Druids were a trpartite system: the BARDI – were singers, the OUVATES – priests and physiologers, and the DRUIDS – physiologer's of ethics and moral learning, the ologers and interpreters of the law and judges in tribal law.

It is also important to understand how the Celts saw the Druids. We know from the classical texts that in the Celtic society the Druids were excused from warfare and did not pay taxes. They were looked to for healing, and the value of their wisdom in both criminal and civil disputes. They operated apart from the tribal leadership as a separate social caste but were the advisors and teachers to the tribal heirarchy....

Caesar, Commentarii de Bello Gallico, VI, 16
'The whole nation of the Gauls is greatly devoted to ritual observances, and for that reason those who are smitten with the more grievous maladies and who are engaged in the perils of battle either sacrifice human victims or vow to do so, employing the Druids as ministers for such sacrifices. They believe, in effect, that, unless for a man's life a man's life be paid, the majesty of

the immortal gods may not be appeased; and in public, as in private, life they observe an ordinance of sacrifices of the same kind. Others use figures of immense size, whose limbs, woven out of twigs [the Wicker Man], they fill with living men and set on fire, and the men perish in a sheet of flame. They believe that the execution of those who have been caught in the act of theft or robbery or some crime is more pleasing to the immortal gods; but when the supply of such fails they resort to the execution even of the innocent'.

Clearly from this commentary it is the Chieftains and Kings who are the ones who decided the punishments, and it was the Druids who were been chosen to carry out the sentences in ritual form. As Caesar stated, the Druid teachings were based in Britannia and brought back to Gaul, so it is fair to accept that the social system and function of the Druids in Gaul and Britannia would be very similar; especially considering that their training could take as much as 20 years and all was committed to memory (little lost in understanding or interpretation as there would be from books).

Another aspect of the Druids is their skills in rhetoric: being able calm the fear in men's hearts, raise the spirit in times of war, or stand between two opposing groups and with the use of words, prevent conflict; such is the respect they seem to have among the tribes. This skill was obviously well learned, Diodorus Siculus (Greek historian 90 – 30 BC) wrote '*They* [the Druids] *pay a great regard to their exhortations, not only in the affairs of peace, but even of war, and these are respected both by their friends and enemies. They sometimes step in between two hostile armies, who are standing with their swords drawn and their spears extended ready to engage; and by their eloquence and the power of wisdom, as if by irresistible enchantment they prevent the effusion of blood and the sheathing of the swords, even among the most fierce barbarians'* . *A skill also used by the Chieftains and Kings (who for obvious reasons were more than likely to have been educated by the Druids). Many speeches were attributed to them by the Greek and Roman historians. Tacitus wrote 'The British chieftains, before battle, fly from rank to rank and address their men with animating speeches, tending to inflame their courage, increase their hope and dispel their fears' In the ancient language of Britannia these speeches were called* BROSNICHIY KAH, *translated by Tacitus as* INCITAMENTA BELLI *or 'Incentives to War'.*

As the son of the Catuvellauni Chieftain, Caratacus who had spurred so many into fighting the Romans in Britannia may well have been used this skill when he was allowed to speak in front of the Roman Senate by Emperor Claudius: his expectation would have been being presented to the Roman citizens in a 'Triumphal Parade' as the defeated enemy of Rome, and then to be killed. [As was Vercingetorix years before – king and chieftain of the Arverni tribe, who united the Gauls in a revolt against Roman forces during the last phase of Julius Caesar's Gallic Wars, but surrendered at the Battle of Alesia to save his people].

Tacitus in Annals, 12.37 records his speech ......

'Had my [*Caratacus*] *moderation in prosperity been equal to my noble birth and fortune, I should have entered this city as your friend rather than your captive; and you would not have disdained to receive, under a treaty of peace, a king descended from illustrious ancestors and ruling many nations. My present lot is as glorious to you as it is degrading to myself. I had men and horses, arms and wealth. What wonder if I parted with them reluctantly? If you Romans chose to lord it over the world, does it follow that the worlds to accept slavery? Were I to have been once delivered up as a prisoner, neither my fall nor your triumph would have become famous. My punishment would be followed*

by oblivion, whereas if you save my life, I shall be an everlasting memorial of your clemency'.

According to the classical texts, he made such an impression on Emperor Claudius and the Senate that he was pardoned and he and his family were allowed to live in peace in Rome (presumably he was not allowed to return to Britannia).

The Druid's position within the tribal structure, their function with regard to criminal and judicial matters, and their rhetoric skills in turning the minds of men by acting as peace makers or strengthening their resolve has already been covered but they were also involved in religion, science, healing and medicines.

They were truly tied into the beliefs of Celtic society; the Celts saw a clear connection between the art of healing and religious rites and which was most effective when they were combined, believing also that the internal diseases of the body were the 'embodiment' of the anger of the gods. It is quite probable that this belief system was expanded upon and the led to the rise in the number of magical rites and incantations used in 'medicinal' practices by the Druids (to heal body and soul) which would have increased their standing even more so in this society.

A small insight into the Druid and their part in Celtic society can be seen with the discovery of the **'Druid of Colchester'** by archaeologists in 1996. The find, at the village of Stanway near Colchester (Camulodunum, in the tribal land of the Catuvellauni), is believed to be a grave of an Iron Age Druid circa. 40-60 AD. It was found among a number of graves of eminent people, believed to have been buried around the time of the Roman invasion of Britain in 43 AD. Within a wooden chambered burial site, archaeologists uncovered cremated human remains, a cloak decorated with brooches, a jet bead believed to have magical properties, medical equipment, a tea strainer still containing some kind of herbal brew, and some mysterious metal rods. The medical equipment consisted of 13 instruments including scalpels, sharp and blunt retractors, needles, a probe, surgical saw, hooks and foreceps. A cup was also found with traces of Mugwort. Some people suggest that herbs, such as Mugwort were smoked to stimulate psychic powers. The tea strainer also contained herbs commonly associated with herbal remedies in ancient times such as artemisia pollen. Healing is an attribute given to druids but there is no clue as to what the metal rods could have been used for; possibly divining?. What is clear though that whoever this person was they were held in high regard given the items they were buried with, possibly an advisor to Cunobelinus the Catuvellauni Chieftain at that time?

There are also classical texts regarding the Druids intricate knowledge of astronomy. Many of their recorded rituals (by Greeks and Romans) were based on the phases of the moon and the alignments. There is also comment on their understanding of Geometry; Pythagorean principles are similar to those of the Druids, which raises the question as to them being involved at some point in time with the stone structures that dot the landscape. Were the Druids involved in such matters or were these from a time before and the geometry knowledge had been passed down?

Whatever the answer was, what is surely evident is that the Druids in whatever role they took within the society whether as teachers, poets, advisers, philosophers, arbitrators, practitioners of healing, makers of herbal medicines, the font of tribal history, astronomers, mathematicians and the leaders of religious rites, or executioners (to name but a few) these individuals really were a valuable resource, as their skills may well have attributed to the success of the tribe to which they were linked.

There are accounts that associate the Druids with the building of stone structures (e.g.henges, standing stones and tombs), but in truth these megalithic structures were built 100's, if not a 1000 years before the Druid's were first recorded circa 300 BC (carbon dating having given us at least a reasonable dateline for materials found at these sites). Some may have been used by the Druids for specific ceremonies that had already been handed down through the ages. If it were true, then why would they not have had their own ritual sites built of stone rather than using the natural sites of groves (Welsh: Llwyn) of Oak etc?

There are places that can be identified as 'Groves' (Welsh: Derlwyn – Oak Grove) on Ordinance Survey publications of Anglesey, Gwynedd and Clwyd, which may indicate some relevance to the past but there is no archaeological evidence to support that they were Druid Groves,......... for example:

Bryn Celli Ddu, Anglesey.. *'The Hill of the Black Grove'*

Llwyn: NW of Tomen y Mur, Gwynedd... *'The Grove'*

Llwyn Crwn: SE of Tomen y Mur, Gwynedd... *'The Round* Grove'

[**Note** Tomen-y-Mur was also the site of a Roman Fort]

Llwyngwril: Meirionnydd, Gwynedd..... *'The Grove of the Brave'*

Llwyndyrys: Llŷn Peninsula, Gwynedd..... *'The Intricate or Difficult Grove'*

Llwynmawr: S of Llangollen, Clwyd..... *'The Great Grove'*

Having reasonably established the Druids position and role within the 'Celtic' tribal system, the question raises itself yet again as to why there is so little mention of them in regard to their role (or lack of it) with the tribes who had allied themselves to Rome (and those who were eventually brought, by force, into the Roman 'fold'). Would these 'Romanised' chieftains have dismissed these supposedly important individuals so quickly from their society and if they did, then how was it done in such a way as to have no reaction from the general population?.In all the classical texts that the author has researched there are no references to the Britannia Druids taking up arms against the Romans, speaking out against them, and inciting the British tribes to fight and carry on the resistance against Roman rule. There are no defining moments recorded that indicate why the Roman leaders in Britannia would have instigated or initiated the 'Paulinus attack' directly at the Druids of MONA INSULIS with such ferocity.

Neither is there any texts of the period that record why the Druids chose Mona as their 'training center' to train those who came to them willingly to the ways of the Druids. Could it have been because the island was the furthest west they could go in order to get the peace and sanctity for study and learning, but still be near enough to mainland Britannia and Gaul so as not to lose contact?. There were certainly Druids in Hibernia(Ireland), who may well have sailed to and from Mona, but it may well have been too far for a Druid centre of learning. The lack of written records by the Druid's means its unlikely we will never know. What is not in dispute is that the Romans believed it to a base for Druidic teaching.

Caesar, Commentarii de Bello Gallico 6.13

'These Druids, at a certain time of the year, meet within the borders of the Carnutes [the Celtae region between the Loire and Seine rivers in France], *whose territory is reckoned as the centre of all Gaul, and sit in conclave in a consecrated spot. Thither assemble from every side all that have disputes, and they*

obey the decisions and judgements of the Druids. It is believed that their rule of life was discovered in Britain and transferred thence to Gaul;and today those who would study the subject more accurately journey, as a rule, to Britain to learn it'.

What stands out in this statement is that Britannia was clearly now just the training centre for the Druids and the real power of the Druid's resided in Europe, and, importantly, it did not mention whether British Druids attended this meeting. It begs the question that if the Gauls and Celts were already under the Roman yoke and had basically neutralised Druid influence there, then why attack the training centre in Britannia if its influence was already on the wane?

A clue as to the real intention of the attack was, may be postulated from a comment Tacitus makes in his *Annals* 14.29, *'Britannia is now in the hands of Seutonius Paulinus, who in military knowledge and in popular favour, which allows no one to be without a rival, vied with his colleague Gnaeus Domitius Corbulo, and aspired to equal his glory of the recovery of Armenia by the subjugation of Rome's enemies. He therefore prepared to attack the island of Mona which had a powerful population and was a refuge for fugitives'*. Yet another text also seems to strengthen the argument: Tacitus notes in Agricola, 14. when commenting on the actions of Paulinus in Britannia .... *'Then Suetonius Paullinus enjoyed success for two years; he subdued several tribes and strengthened our military posts. Thus encouraged, he made an attempt on the island of Mona, as a place from which the rebels drew reinforcements'* ... yet again no mention of the Druids!

The action Seutomius Paulinus was planning to undertake was not about the Druids at all, it was about breaking what Paulinus saw as the last bastion of resistance (in Britannia) at this time to Rome (there is no record of resistance or aggression to the Romans in the lands to the north of the Brigantes at this time) and significantly, by achieving success he would gain huge military renown and political favour with the Emperor, which Tacitus suggests he craved. This is more akin to using a 'sledgehammer to crack a nut'.

Interestingly it begs another equally important question; why were the 'fugitives' fleeing to Ynys Môn and from where?? With the lack of any relevant information from either contemporary records or from other classical texts of the period, any answer can only be a matter of conjecture.

The Druids were an integral part of the Celtic society, so it is logical to expect that the local populations would have looked to them in times of turmoil (as have civilisations through the centuries looked to their religious leaders for comfort and succour). So displaced by or fleeing from the Romans, it is likely they would go to the Druids 'homeland' of Ynys Mon, as far away from the soldiers and veterans as possible. The island would have been more suitable for arable farming (the soils were good enough to grow the spelt wheat, and even emmer wheat on the poorer soils) than the mountains of Clwyd, Berwyn and Snowdonia. It was also known to have been trading with Hibernia, amongst others, via its ports. It could therefore have sustained a reasonable population without too much difficulty and with little or no interference from the Romans. The mainland 'homesteads' may have been able to accommodate these displaced people for a short period of time but none appear to have been of any size to cope for a longer period. The Tre'r Ceiri settlement seems to have been the only community that showed any growth in its around this period though not necessarily because of the Romans.

What were they fleeing from is a more difficult

question to determine. It is is reasonable to assume that they would have come from the lands of the Deceangli, whose hill forts were being taken apart by Roman troops as part of the 'Romanisation process. The Ordovician territories close to the border with the Cornovii would have had more frequent incursions by Roman troops and Auxiliaries (especially with the X1111 Legion now based at Viroconium and Auxiliary troops housed in smaller forts along the 'border'). It is also quite possible that disaffected Celts came from further afield in Britannia, believing that they were at least safe from the Roman advances and destruction of settlements. The people themselves would have been warriors, families and survivors of Roman actions. These dispossessed groups may well have been a breeding ground and source for new 'warriors' to carry on the fight against the Roman forces as was suggested by Tacitus.

There is no suggestion in any of the texts that a rebel army was being armed and trained on the island ready for a direct assault against Roman troops or even that a well trained band of Celts had opposed the Romans as they marched all the way to the Menai Strait before fleeing across the water to safety. With nothing else to substantiate the force that was to oppose Paulinus's troops other than the description by Tacitus of '*... the opposing army with its dense array of armed warriors, while between the ranks dashed women, in black attire like Furies, with hair dishevelled, waving brands. All around, the Druids, lifting up their hands to heaven and pouring forth dreadful imprecations...*' it is quite conceivable that the 'army' facing the Romans was nothing more than large group of fugitives, men and women fighting for their very lives and not a warrior army as Tacitus suggests. In all honesty, given the fighting outfits of most of the Brythonic Celts, it would be very difficult to determine from across the Menai Strait, a band of Celtic warriors or a band of farmers (with any weapon they could find) trying to defend their families and themselves, with the Druids calling for help from the Gods. The *Welsh* Celtic God and Goddess of war where Llasar Llaesgyfnewid and his wife Cymidei Cymeinfoll: Andrastae was the Celtic goddess of war.

A significant point which does not appear to have been raised prominently by historians regarding the Druids; possibly because of the limited references in the historical texts is that of female Druids. In the extraxct above Tacitus mentions *'amongst the ranks dashed women in black attire, like Furies'*. Females did have prominent roles within Celtic society and therfore more than likely to have been represented in the Druidic system. He clearly identified them by their 'uniform' suggesting that they were not part of the general populus but rather with the Druids and their role in this case was to incite insults against the Roman troops or call down the wrath of the Celtic goddesses on these 'invaders'. Could these women be Druidesses, prophetesses and diviners... the ancestors of the *wrach* (translated from the Welsh as *witch*) who would appear in ancient welsh folklore as having great knowledge of herbs and medicines, as well as having the gift of prophesy.

There is little mention of Druidesses contemporary to the 1st Century AD but there are records in 3rd Century texts by Lampridius (Alex.Severus, LIX, 5), Voscopius (Numerianus, XIV and Aurelianus, XLIII, 4, 5) all relating to events involving female Druids in Gaul, but nothing in Britannia.

In the Irish Celtic tale, *Táin Bó Cúailnge* (*trans.as* The Cattle Raid of Cooley) there is a specific mention of a Fedelm (a prophetess and seer from Sid Cruachna) who had been away in Britannia, learning the arts of prophesy and

Druidism. She was brought before the great queen of Connacht, Queen Medb, and asked to make a prophesy.

The research has also highlighted the fact that not all the Druids followed the non-violence route. In Irish Celtic tales there are more than a few instances of their Druids recorded as being physically involved in fighting against other tribes. The Celtic influence stretched from Galatia (Anatolya in modern day Turkey) in the east to Hibernia in the west so it is likely that different tribes may have made more demands on their Druids than others.

With all this in mind it does beg the question as to how the Druids viewed themselves and what was their function in the land in which they lived. Were they a religious or a sectarian group trained to be the repository of a cultural identity based on a specific social and spiritual belief system that bound the tribal units in which they lived together and acted as the 'keystone' for its continuance?. Religion tends to be defined more as a spiritual context for the body and soul where as Druidism appears to have been much more than that; involving community law and punishment, health, music, poetry and the recorders of the ancestral lines and identity.

The 20 years of training that the Druids undertook was without the written word, meaning that all that knowledge was memorised, and believed to have been done by using rhyming poetry – clearly a definitive link to the poetry of the Bards. Greek and Roman historians believed that the Druids had the ability to remember vast amounts of information. However it was was also the achilles heel for the Druids, with the death of a Driud the knowledge was lost forever. Unlike the Romans who brought the written word to Britannia making the 'transmission' of information, facts and memories much easier to be retained and read by a wider audience for generations to come.

The Campaign to MONA: AD 60

In his 5th Century treatise *'Eptima rei militaris'* (Epitome of the Art of War) Publius Flavius Vegetius Renatus (commonly known as Vegetius) when discussing Roman warfare of military principles of methods and practices during the height of the Roman Empire, stated that the success of the Roman war machine was in the *'training of disciplined soldiers, orderly strategy, maintenance of supply lines and logistics, quality of leadership and the use of tactics'* These would probably have been the precepts by which Paulinus would have based his campaign plan.

The initial starting point has to be going back to Tacitus' description of what occurred on the shores of the Menai Strait and nowhere else on the island. This is important, as there is a clear inference that this was a land based attack and the Romans only reached the island by crossing the Strait. It can therefore interpreted that no Roman Naval warships or large transports were used to land Roman troops elsewhere on Mona. Large expansive beaches and low lying land on the SW and NE coast of the island would have been ideal for a co-ordinated attack.

The key objective appears to have been to break the Ordovician resistance. They would have had to go through their heartland using only trackways (there were no roads) attacking enemy forces as they moved forward to the main centre of resistance, Mona. It had to be a land based attack through their lands to accomplish this crushing any resistance as they moved forward to their main objective. A sea based attack on the island could have seen many of the 'resistance' fighter and Druids escape across to the mainland and disappear into the mountains to carry on the 'fight' for decades. It is also true to say that Paulinus would have had difficulty in getting Roman troops (in battle order) to board ships and land on the island beaches. Even if they had embarkation ports along the coast they had a record of resisting such ventures (crossing the English Channel). Bad weather could also have easily put paid to those plans also. It is quite probable that Governor Paulinus took only a few months to decide that he 'needed' to act against Mona, especially when after taking command he found that the previous Governors had failed to subdue the tribes of this region and crush any resistance.

In order to facilitate the right platform for the attack (as has already been covered in a previous chapter) he established a permanent Legion fort at Viroconium for the XIIII Legion drawing in its cohorts already spread out in legionary vexillation forts established by his predecessors at Manduessedum, Letocetum, Wall, Drayton Lodge, Pennocrucium, Streton Mill, Vxacona, and Viroconium. He then had Auxiliary troops moved up to this region from the south and east to occupy the vacated vexillation forts while he built up his force for the coming campaign.

As far as the rest of the Britannia 'controlled' by the Romans: the II Augusta (based in Isca) had subdued most of the south west of Britannia and forts were being erected to maintain peace (at the time of Seutonius's attack on Mona, praefectus castorum Poenius Potumus was in charge, there is no record as to where the Legion's Legate was); XX Legion, based in Glevum, was moving further into south west Wales and maintaining order; VIIII Legion (under Legate Quintus Petillius Ceralis) based in Lindum Colonia had a watching brief on the *Brigantes* to the North, and the Colonias had cohorts of veteran Roman troops acting as a 'police' force. To all intents and purposes it was peaceful enough, forces were in place should anything happen. In this belief Paulinus could move forward against Mona.

The Legion most appropriate and closest to *Ordovices* territory and therefore central to the campaign, in all matters of logistics, was the XIIII Legion based in vexillation forts (normally manned by single cohorts) at Manduessedam along the eastern border of Ordovician lands in the land of the Cornovii. The Legion would have already been gaining good intelligence on the lay of the land from incursions and patrols into the mountains and valleys, and probable skirmishes with the tribesmen (ref page 64 regarding population distribution along the border region)

As has been mentioned earlier, Paulinus' experience of fighting in mountainous terrain (Atlas Mountains) gave him a head start when planning his campaign against the hill tribes of western Britannia;

Historical note: *Current records and archaeological evidence suggest that there was no Roman Fort at Deva until the AD 70's so there would have been no Roman Naval support from any base on the west coast of Britannia until then. Most of the Roman naval forces were still based on the south coast acting as miltary transports/protection for goods, materials and men from Gaul to Britannia and vice versa.*

He also had the advantage of the tactical knowledge of the terrain the terrain he would be entering, from those military commanders who had already carried out full scale attacks into the territory under the campaigns of Scapula and Didius. With this knowledge he could establish the forces he would use to move forward, what water sources would be available for his troops and animals and the modes of transport he would require to make the journey. It is also likely that he would have utilised some of ala units (cavalry) based at the forts to 'scout' further into the region and search out established track ways as well as calling on the knowledge of local traders who dealt with the tribesmen.

The key point about moving such a large force of soldiers, equipment and supplies is that they needed to ensure that they had enough to feed the men and animals, and have access to a continuous supply to a good water.

This would have had several implications on the planning of this campaign:

Timing: The Roman armies campaigning was done during the period that Rome considered was their Summer – mid May to mid August when the weather would have been most favourable and food and forage for the animals would be in plentiful supply.

Least arduous route to man, animals and carts:
valley bottoms rather than over hills and mountains thus minimising fatigue and achieving good daily marching distances.

Shortest practical route:
reducing the requirement for vast quantities of food to be carried.

Accessible water supply-utilising natural rivers and lakes along as much of the route as possible:
this is essential, especially in a hostile environment - human and animal daily requirements will be discussed under Logistics.

Having up to date information on the type of enemy forces they would come up against, the terrain and what major obstacles would be in the way (in this case the Menai Strait) made the devising of the route based on all these parameters easier for Paulinus to choice of men and materials required for the campaign.

The Campaign Troops
There is nothing in the classical records that states which actual troop formations (Legion, Vexillation and Auxiliaries) were brought together for this campaign. The following is surmised from what formations he brought back from Mona to deal with the Boudicca uprising (which is recorded), and what forces would have been available to him en route with minimal impact to the rest of Roman controlled Britannia. The figure of 10,000 men was recorded by Tacitus Annals.14.34 on his return from Mona to meet Boudicca and her forces – after 'sweeping up' veterans of the XX Legion and auxiliaries on route to boost his forces.

In 'Nero's Killing Machine: XIV Legion' by Stephen Dando Collins (2005), he identifies Seutonius as delaying his march back to Camulodunum in order to draw in more forces so that when he met with Boudicca and her army, *'he had the XIIII Legion, 2.000 veterans of the XX Legion (many possibly serving in the militia's), 2,000 Batavian Auxiliaries and 1,000 cavalry split between the Batavian Horse Regiment and the 1st Wing of Thracian Horse'*.

Authors Note: 2,000 veteran's of the Legio XX collected en route does seem a very large figure especially when most veterans would in all probablility have stayed in the region where they had been based (Camulodunum from c. AD 50 – 55, when it was transferred to the R Usk in South Wales (neither of which were en route from the island.) It is more likely that veterans were picked up and co-opted into the Legio XX vexillation returning from Mona with Paulinus.

The general composition of the Legions and the Auxilia

Legionary rank (ascending order	**Number in legion**	**Role**	**Auxilia equivalent: *cohortes and ala****
Contubernium	5,120	infantryman	pedes (eques)*
Cornicen	59	horn-blower	cornicen
Tesserarius	59	officer of the watch	tesserarius (sesquiplicarius)*
Optio	59	centurion's deputy	optio (duplicarius)*
Signifer	59	*centuria* standard-bearer	signifer
Imaginifer	1	bearer of emperor's image	vexillarius
Aquilifer	1	legion standard-bearer	
			- - - - (curator)*
Centurio	45	centurion	centurio (decurio)*
Centurio primi ordinis	13 (9 pilus prior + 4 1st Cohort)	senior centurion	centurio princeps (decurio princeps)*
Centurio primus pilus(1)	1	senior centurion	none
Tribunus militum angusticlavius	5	legion staff-officer	praefectus auxilii - regimental commander
Praefectus castrorum	1	legion quartermaster (executive officer to legatus)	none
Tribunus militum laticlavius	1	legion deputy commander	none
Legatus legionis	1	legion commander	none

The standing force of the Legion at this time would have been around 5,400 men, which included administrators and servants.

The Roman Army

Roman legionaire with his marching kit
(Wikimedia Commons)

Before 107 BC Rome had a seasonal army of only trained men who owned land and they fought for a year before they were allowed to return home. However, when faced with the powerful Numidians, Gaius Marius (a general in the Roman Republic) knew that changes would need to be made if Rome was to be victorious. He set about making serious reforms to the Roman army: any Roman citizen could now join (not just landowners), they would be paid, be given standard uniforms and equipment. They would sign on for 15-20 years, become a member of a fully functional standing army and be allowed to enjoy the spoils of war... there was no problem in recruiting after this [known as the Marian Reforms]

As a legionnaire he was part of a well trained, disciplined, cohesive and effective force that was well versed in the art of war. They had a wealth of defensive and offensive tactics that led to their military dominanace over their enemies. They were difficult to beat... but not impossible. The individual soldier had a good range of personal weapons (all of which was standardised throughout the Roman army) at his disposal and after he had undertaken rigorous training in their use. He fought not as an individual, but a member of a century unit and the legion in a formidable military machine.

Roman soldiers had fought many battles against very different foes over the centuries as they were expanding their empire initially for the Republic and then for the Empire. When they came across new weapons and tactics they believed were of great advantage to their army, they were adopted into the Roman army. They also were not averse to 'inviting' defeated tribes to form Auxilia units if they had qualities the Roman army could use, rather than form new distinct units of the Roman Legions i.e. Thracian light cavalry, Batavians who could swim rivers in full armour.

When Caesar fought the Celts in Gaul he found the tribesmen using shorter swords (around 50 cm in length) behind their shield wall. These proved to be ideal for stabbing at their opponents from behind the shield rather than opening up to slash with longer swords as the Romans were doing (swords around 71 cm). Caesar quickly learnt the lesson and the Roman army adopted the shorter sword which was even more effective in the Roman soldiers trained hand.

Personal Weapons

Pugio – Dagger

It had a large leaf-shaped blade 18 to 28 cm long and 5 cm or more wide and was worn on the left side. The hilt was 10–12 cm long overall (often decorated with inlaid silver) and the grip was quite narrow; producing a very secure grip.

Gladius – Sword

Worn high on the right side it enabled the soldier to draw it underarm with his right hand without interfering with the position of the shield in his left hand (another advantage of the shorter 50 cm - 60 cm or 24 inches – sword) and remain safely behind it.

Scutum – Shield

Was a large rectangular curved shield weighing approximately 10 kg (22 lbs) which was made of 3 sheets of wood glued together, covered in canvas and leather (a thickness of 5-6 mm), with a central spindle-shaped boss (an umbo) and a metal rim around the edge of the shield. It made for ideal protection against missiles as the shape made it easy to interlink them into a defensive screen above their heads (the Testudo) when moving forwards and when dismantling lose stone ramparts barring their way. The metal rim also proved a good weapon, as when using the shields as a wall to 'punch' forwards against their opponents in close combat they could be slammed down on their opponents exposed feet.

Pilum – Throwing spear

The Roman soldier was issued with 2 spears on the battle line and these would be launched against the enemy before close combat ensued. They were about 2 metres in length weighing between 2 and 4 kg (4 – 8 lbs), and consisted of a wooden shaft from which projected an iron shaft about 7 mm in diameter and 60cm long ending in a pyramidal shaped head. It was designed to penetrate both shield and armour, to wound the enemy or at the very least prevent the enemy from using his shield effectively. It would have weighed it down and even when the wooden shaft broke off (which it was designed to do easily) it still left the iron shaft bent in his shield and making it unwieldy.

Entrenching Tools

The Roman soldier on the march would have been expected to dig a ditch and construct a rampart around their camp each night when established camps were not available. These tools – e.g. the shovel (batillium) and the pickaxe or mattock (dolabra) - would have been useful as improvised weapons if the user was attacked and could not reach his usual weapons.

Tribulus - Caltrop

Was made up of two or more sharp nails fashioned together into four spikes or points arranged so that in whatever manner it was thrown on the ground, it rested on three and presents the fourth in a stable upright position. Caltrops were used as part of the defences that served to slow the advance of enemy soldiers, cavalry or horse-drawn chariots by impaling feet or hooves. They could be easily carried in a leather satchel and strewn on the ground in front of them or around the outside of a marching camp in hostile territory.

Personal Armour

Galea (*Coolus type*) – Helmet

A metal (commonly brass) helmet which had a raised neck peak to eye level and a sturdy frontal peak on the brow and cheek pieces which could be tied together beneath the chin.

Lorica segmentata - Body Armour -

The armour itself consisted of broad ferrous strips ('girth hoops') fastened to internal leather straps. The strips were arranged horizontally on the body, overlapping downwards, and they surrounded the torso in two halves, being fastened at the front and back by means of brass hooks, which were joined by leather laces.The upper body and shoulders were protected by additional strips ('shoulder guards') and breast and backplates. The form of the armour allowed it to be stored very compactly since it was possible to separate it into four sections

Lorica Hamata **- a type of chain mail armour.**
It was comprised of alternating rows of closed washer-like rings punched from iron sheets and rows of riveted rings made from drawn wire that ran horizontally, producing very flexible, reliable and strong armour. Iit was the preferred armour of the auxilia and the centurions because of its greater coverage and lower maintenance. Though variations were intoduced these remained in constant use by legionaries.

The Roman Soldiers Marching Pack
The pack included a number of items suspended from a **Furca**(**e**) or carrying pole. Items carried in the pack included:

- ***Loculus***: a leather satchel
- Waterskin: Roman camps would primarily be built near water sources but each soldier would have to carry his water for the day's march in a waterskin.
- Food: each legionary would carry some of his food. Although a Roman army on the move would typically have a baggage train of mules or similar to carry supplies such as food: legionaries were required to carry about 15 days worth of basic food supplies with them.
- Cooking equipment: including a cooking pot, a skewer and a ***Patera*** – a broad, shallow dish used for drinking.
- Entrenching tools: Carried by legionaries to construct fortifications and dig latrines etc. Each legionary

would typically carry either a shovel or pickaxe for digging, a turf cutting tool or a wicker basket for hauling earth.
- *Sudes:* stakes for construction of the camps defence (vallum).

Roman Heavy Weapons

Seutonius would have taken mobile weapons with him or would have had the materials to construct them once he had established his encampment near to the Menai Strait shore. There would have been no need for siege equipment such as the Onager (catapult) though projectiles could have been fired across the Strait at its narrowest point bur some may have been taken. He was out to destroy the fugitives and the Druids as quickly as possible, so mobility and quick fire would have been the preferred option.

Ballista

A powerful crossbow powered by torsion in bundles of sinew rather than torsion in the arms. Early versions projected heavy darts called bolts, fire arrows or spherical stone projectiles of various sizes to a distance of about 500 m (later versions up to a 1000m) at an eleveated trajectory and with a firing rate of 2 bolts per min. They were also mounted on a cart and called a carroballista (mobile artillery). These would have been easy to construct at the battle site.

Scorpio

Was the smaller version of the Ballista. A torsion-powered crossbow-like weapon that fired smaller arrows and was used for precision fire and also for parabolic shooting. It fired bolts capable of piercing enemy shields and armour to kill and injure enemy troops and a similar firing rate as the ballista (up to 3/4 bolts per minute). They were so-named for their deadly, armour-piercing 'sting' and could be operated by just one or two men. Thanks to their smaller size they could also be mounted on the back of wagons or flat-bottomed boats.

From the 1st Century BC, the Roman army supplied each Legion with 60 ballista/scorpio machines. If all were deployed on the battlefield there would be a minimum of 120 bolts per minute raining down on the enemy, a serious amount of fire power.

When not on campaign the legions (and Auxilia) were deployed into detachments called Vexillations (normally a cohort) and would march under a square cloth banner called a Vexillum which bore the units number, title and emblem. These troops would be manning border forts. Their role was to 'police' the eastern region they were responsible for, gathering intelligence not only about the landscape (for mapping) and road building but also and making incursions and intelligence gathering into 'enemy' territory.

Though not an extensive description of the troops and equipment available to Seutonius as he prepared his march to MONA, this information demonstrates what sort of force was believed to have been brought against the ***'powerful force of fugitives and Druids'*** residing on this island in the west that so threatened the Roman presence in Britannia. This was an experienced standing army with advanced weapons for both close quarter and longer range fighting, who had already come up against the Britons of the lowlands in battle so knew what type of battle they would be facing.

Training and Skills

A Roman soldier was not only required to be fully trained in the use of his personal weapons but function as part of a well disciplined army unit (punishment was extremely harsh for failure to be so). They would also trained to use heavy weapons such as the Ballista, the Scorpio and the Onagar. The soldier must also be able to turn his hand to most things in order for the Legion to function with no outside support, especially on campaign. These would include such things as:

- carpenters
- labourers
- administrators
- manufacurers (blacksmiths)
- engineers
- builders

.... basically any role required of them by the legion.

The 1st Century AD Jewish General and historian, Flavius Josephus, described the training of the Roman legions as *'bloodless battles and their battles as bloody drills. Every soldier was exercised every day, which is why they bear fatigue of battle so easily'*.

There weree 2 Roman legions refered to as possibly being involved in Paulitus' attack on Mona and would more than likey have had Auxiliary troops also involved.

Legio X1111
Gemina Martia)

The emblem of the legion was the 'sea goat' Capricorn, as where many of the Legions raised by Caesar. Their sheild device was the thunderbolt of Jupiter with

Legion X1111 emblem
(Wikimedia Commons)

wings. It was the only legion to do so in the same manner as the Praetorian Guard.

He (Julius Caesar) recruited the XIIII Legion in 57 BC during the Gallic wars and deployed them in battle against the Nervians in Cispalpine Gaul. In the same year, the legion was set against Ambiorix and the Eburones of Belgium where they were virtually annihilated but due to the actions of the the Legion Aquilifer, Lucius Petrosidus, they did not lose the Legions Aquila (Eagle) Standard, so Caesar was able to immediately reform the Legion. It saw action again at the siege of Alesia in 52 BC (the final battle against the tribes of Gaul and the capture of their leader Vercingetorix).

In the Civil War between Caesar and Pompey the Great, the legion fought for Caesar in the battle of Ilerda in Hispania and saw action again in the battle of Pharsalus in 48 BC. The legion was reinforced with the disbanded legions of the defeated Mark Anthony by Octavian (who was to become Emperor Augustus) after the Battle of Actium. It was at this point that the cognomen ***Gemina*** (twinned) was added to the Legion's Battle Standard.

In 21 BC, the legion was sent out to suppress the rebellion of the Turoni in Gaul, who had revolted against the heavy Roman taxation under two noblemen named Julius Sacrovir and Julius Florus.

The next campaign for the legion was in 6 BC against King Maroboduus of the Marcomanni in Czechia which took three years; as the Roman forces also had to put down a revolt in Pannonia to finish the task. For their service in this campaign the Legion cognomen on the standard was changed to ***Gemina Martia*** (twinned and martial).

Note: *Following the defeat and Boudicca and her forces in AD 61 by the 'valiant actions' of the XIIII Legio it was rewarded with the honorific title of* **Victrix** *('victorious, blessed by Mars').*

Then, the Romans were defeated and humiliated in the Teutoberg Forest in Germania (September AD 9). During the re-shuffling of the Roman forces after this disaster the legion was transferred to Mogontiacum (Mainz), a Roman fort on the west bank of the river Rhine (and provincial capital of Germania Superior), where it shared a base with XVI Gallica.

In the winter of AD 40 - 41, the legion was in action against the Chatti near Mainz in Caligula's war against the Germania tribes.

By AD 43 it had been brought to the coast of Gaul along with 3 other Legions to invade Britannia (the standing force of the Legion at this time would have been around 5,400 men). Prior to AD 60 they had already fought both the *Decangli* and the *Ordovices* under previous Governors of Britannia.

In AD 60 this Legion was actively based in Viroconium

Legio XX

It is possible that a vexillation of the Legio XX was assigned to the Legio XIIII for the campaign but it is not possible to confirm – this belief is based on the historical texts recounting the troops Paulinus took with him when he went to meet Boudicca and her supporters in battle. According to the historical evidence the Legio XX were based in South Wales so would not have been collected up on route by Paulinus in his rush to prevent further catastrophy. It would be reasonable to

Legion XX emblem
Attribution to author CatMan61

surmise that he had taken the vexillation with him to Mona.

The legion was thought to have been founded shortly after 31 BC by the emperor Augustus and formed part of the large Roman force that fought in the final stages of the Cantabrian Wars in north west Hispania from 25 to 19 BC.

The legion then moved to Burnum in Illyricum at the beginning of the Pannonian uprising in AD 6. Whilst there, they were led by the governor of Illyricum, Marcus Valerius Messalla Messallinus who may have given his clan (gens) name Valeria to the legion, so that it now had the cognomen ***Valeria Victrix***. Although understrength, they managed to defeat the rebels led by Bato of the Daesitates. In one battle the legion cut through the enemy lines, was surrounded, and cut its way out again.

It may well have been operating alongside the Legio XIIII when it was moved again against the Marcomanni in Czechia in AD 6. With this legion too, after the Teutoberg Forest disaster in AD 9, it was moved to Germania Inferior and based at Oppidium Ubiorum (Cologne) then moved to Novaesium (the site of modern day Neuss) to strengthen the border against the Germanic tribes who lay to the east of the Rhine.

By AD 43 it too had been brought to the coast of Gaul along with 3 other Legions for the invasion of Britannia. As has already been noted, this legion had fought against the *Silures* and the *Ordovices* including the final battle against Caratacus at Caer Caradog.

In AD 60 this Legion was split between it headquarters at Glevum and a secondary fort on the river Usk.

Auxiliary Troops: The Auxilia

These first appeared under Emperor Augustus, regiments of about 500 strong, a tenth the size of a Roman legion. They were recruited from the peregrini or non-citizen inhabitants of the empire who constituted approximately 90 percent of the Empire's population in the 1st century AD. It is likely that tribal kings or chieftains, conquered by or allied to Rome to show good faith and obedience to the Emperor they would have supplied men to form these Auxilla units to fight alongside Roman troops in other provinces than their own (for obvious reasons). The auxilia provided virtually all the army's cavalry (there were only 120 Roman cavalry troops per legion), light infantry, archers and other specialists, in addition to heavy infantry equipped in a similar manner to legionaries.

There were three basic types of auxiliary regiments:

- ***Ala:*** contained only cavalry and consisted nominally of 480 soldiers
- ***Cohortes peditatae***, or simply cohors: contained only infantry and consisted nominally of 480 soldiers
- ***Cohortes equitatae: ala:*** contained infantry with an attached cavalry contingent and consisted nominally of 600 soldiers, of which 480 were infantry and 120 were cavalry

A number of regiments, of all three types, had designated *sagittariorum* (sagittarii) indicating that they specialised archer units within their compliment.

In Britannia at this time the records both text and by archeological evidence show that the Auxilla were made up primarily of:

Thracian - cavalry (ala)
Batavians – cohortes and ala

In the period between 30 BC and AD 68 there was a transformation of the Auxilia from groups of trained men to a standing corps with standardised structure, equipment and conditions of service. By the end of this period the changes put in place would have significantly increased the Roman armies military and combat strength. There were no significant differences between legionaries and auxiliaries in terms of training and thus combat capability. The proportion of auxiliaries in Britannia in AD 69 was approximately 50% of the Roman force.

Under the emperor Claudius, a minimum term of 25 years' service was established for auxiliary service and on completion of the term auxiliary soldiers, and their children were from this time routinely granted Roman citizenship as a reward for service [folding bronze tablets engraved with the soldiers services record or military diploma exist from the time of Emperor Claudius and could be used to prove their Roman citizenship]. Claudius also decreed that prefects of auxiliary regiments must all be of equestrian rank, thus excluding centurions from such commands, though indigenous chiefs continued to command some auxiliary regiments (they were normally granted the rank of Roman knight for the purpose).

Rome had learnt through many battles across its empire that it needed to constantly adapt its fighting tactics and where possible use the skills of those who had once opposed them to Rome's advantage. By AD 68 the Auxiliaries formations, armour and weapons were:

Cohortes (**cohorts**) – approximately 500 men
They would have been supplied with the same infantry weapons as the Roman troops but probably with some of their own styles of spears, bows and knives.

Ala – **cavalry** - approximately 500 men
The Roman Auxilia cavalry were usually heavily armoured and armed with a short lance, javelins, the spatha long

sword and sometimes bows for specialist horse archer units. These men served primarily as medium missile cavalry for flanking, scouting, skirmish, and pursuit.

Personal Weapons

Spatha - Sword

Longer one than the Gladius as it was used to slash and thrust at their enemy on the ground or on horseback. They would also have carried a Pugio.

Shields - oval or hexagonal

Would have been used when out scouting in front of or on the flanks of a marching legion, but in battle (or skirmishing and pursuit) it would have impeded the rider by restricting movement and control of both the shield and horse when the other hand held the sword or short lance/javelin. Some of the auxilia would also have been skilled horse bowmen.

Personal Armour

Lorica squamata - armour

A scale body armour shaped in the same way as a lorica hamata, mid-thigh length with the shoulder doublings or cape similar to the legionnaires but was made from small metal scales sewn to a fabric backing. Much more suitable for men on horseback, though the hamata was more widely used because it required little maintenance, constant movement reduced any rusting meaning that it could last at least a decade and only weighed 11 kgs.

Helmet

It was a cavalry version of the infantry helmet with more protective features - such as flaps that completely covered the ears.

An example of a Roman Cavalry Soldier (Wikimedia Commons)

A fragment of lorica squamata scale armour

Skills

The all-mounted ala(e) were the elite cavalry of the army, they were specifically trained in elaborate battle manoeuvres. They were best-suited for large-scale operations and battle, during which they acted as the primary cavalry escort for the legions. During this period the alae were made up of Batavians and Thracians all of whom had long established skills and experience of fighting on horseback.

The Logistics

Based on these facts, it is reasonable to assume that Viroconium was the base at which Seutonius would up his store of food and materials required for the march. It was the nearest Roman base from which to move against the *Ordovicians* and those in active resistance against Rome. His next priority therefore, had to be the establishment of a permanent Legionary fort at Viroconium as opposed to the smaller vexillation and auxiliary forts that were in the surrounding area. It would have to have a robust and effective supply line from his main centres and ports in the south; to this end he had Watling Street extended to the town so that he could commence that build up. The amount of grain required would have been huge, so he would have had to have had it brought in from far and wide on wagons (angarie) drawn by oxen, carrying a typical payload of 650 kgs, to granaries within the vicinity of the Viroconium Legion fort.

The land he was going to be campaigning in was primarily mountains and valleys which would not have been able to supply his troops and animals just through foraging, especially if the 'enemy' had employed a 'scorched earth' policy. Reforms set up under Emperor Augustus put into place a complex supply organisation which enabled an army to campaign in all seasons in enemy territory.

From the fort, the Legion would have had to move its own supplies up to its marching-camps. Based on a number of writings on the subject of Roman military campaigning marching-camps, it required about 1,400 mules to accomplish the movement of sufficient food supplies for a full legion. In addition, each of the legion's 600 *contubernia* (8-man platoons who shared a campaign-tent) had one or two mules to carry its tent and other equipment. The driving of the supply mule-train, and the care of the pack-animals was in the hands of the legion's *calones*, (professional camp-servants most likely also on the army pay-roll) who accompanied the unit everywhere on campaign. These men were armed as light infantry and given basic combat-training so that they could protect the mule-train and, in emergencies, the marching-camp itself. The Legion would have 200-300 *calones* accompanying them (*Calones* were distinct from the personal servants – slaves or freedmen – whom the officers generally took on campaign with them).

Following the Marian reforms (107 BC) of Roman military standards equipment, training and tactics, (which produced a new formidable fighting force) the marching troops would have been be expected to carry their own daily rations (though it was dependant on actual situations, certainly it would have been the case in hostile territoy). Equipment, such as tools and parts for the artillery weapons and stocks of missiles would also have been carried on carts drawn by oxen (the marching camps defences would have been carried on the mules with the *Calones*). There are no clear accounts of what type of artillery pieces were used but as discussed earlier, each legion at this time had 60 scorpios as basic artillery, ballistae could have been carried and reassembled at the battle site and onagers may also have been taken.

The major factor for any army on the move is to keep its men and animals supplied with food and most importantly water. With having such a large force moving through hostile territory the water sources needed to be large and flowing; static water could have been contaminated by the enemy, rivers are much more difficult to affect as it would be detrimental to both sides.

We do not have a clear idea of what the climate was like during this period, but the major valleys on the proposed routes are substantial enough to have had water courses in them then, though smaller water courses may have changed or disappeared over the millenia. So the proposed routes ares based on the likelihood of these current water sources being available then to either a greater or lesser degree. Most Roman military campaigns were carried out during the spring and summer, and to give an indication of what sort of volumes of water that would be required per day. Referring to research on this subject carried out by Steve Kaye (2013), the consumption figures are based on a days marching (the general consensus is that the 'marching day' was from around 7.00am to 3.00pm):

- Soldiers weighed down by approximately 43 kilos of clothing, weapons and a furca, including rations plus their efforts in rampart and ditch digging of the marching fort, foraging and fodder collection.

This figure is based on the work done by Jonathan Roth in his book 'The logistics of the Roman Army at War (264 BC – AD 235)' In it he evaluates data from a variety of sources (both classical and contemporary) concerning what a Roman soldier was expected to carry on a march. Vegetius stated that the soldier was trained to carry burdens (suggesting a heavy weight) and the Marian reforms had standardised a method of bearing equipment in balanced and manageable way so that rest stops would be easy to manage.

The point was proved by the German historian and experimental archaeologist. Marcus Junklemann in 1985 when he successfully led a group of German civilians, dressed as 1st Century legionnaires and each carrying packs of 43-46 kgs, over 500 kms from Verona to Augsburg across the Alps, averaging 25 kms (c.15 miles) per day. They were not athletes but did train individually for the march. So if modern day civilians could do this, then the 1st Century seasoned Roman soldier could certainly do it.

- Calones, personal servants and muleteers
- Contubernium mules carrying weights of up to 145 kgs: their tent (papilio) hand-mill, cooking pot, tools and baskets, and 16 pila muralia/sudis (for the defences of the marching fort) and their rations (normally for 5 days on 1 mule)
- Hard working horses and mules, though oxen may well have been used to pull heavier carts carrying military equipment in this campaign).
- Travelling on structured roads
- Operating in temperatures between 20 and 25 C

This gives a grand total of 132,200 ltrs of water required /day

	Soldiers	***Calones/ Servants Muleteers***	***Horses***	***Mules***
Number of	7000	300	350	1400
ltrs/day each	9	9	70	30
Total (ltrs)/day	63,000	2,700	24,500	42,000

Note: this is just an approximation of consumption, but it does give an idea as to the quantity of water required to sustain a marching column. In the case of this particular campaign to Mona, the demand would have varied considerably: officers would be riding, the men and animals would be travelling along track ways and not Roman roads and the weather (and temperatures), would have been much more changeable travelling through the mountains. It does however indicate that a considerable amount of fresh water was needed to be sourced on route. From the research Steve Kaye (2013) carried out, he found that 90% of the Roman forts that their research covered in Britannia were within 300 mtrs of a water source sufficient to maintain both troops and livestock.

Snowdonia Mountains and Menai Strait from Beaumaris

Plas Newydd

Porthaethwy

The Route (see map overleaf)

There are no records in the classical texts of Tacitus, Cassius Dio or Seutonius that reveal the route Paulinus and his troops took to reach the shores of the Menai Strait. I propose to offer some credible routes across the *Ordovician* territory based on known facts, Roman military tactics used in the 1st century and archaeological evidence that adds weight (but not necessarily confirming) to the most likely route they would have taken. The advent of aerial photography and crop mark observations has brought about the discovery of more marching forts in Britain than ground work ever did. It has expanded our knowledge of the size, construction and positioning of these forts in Wales, as more areas are covered (and in the right conditions) there are probably still more to be found. What is also likely is that some of the temporary marching forts used in various campaigns may have been lost forever due to erosion or farming techniques over the centuries. It does make interpreting campaign routes somewhat difficult as any proposition regarding a specific route would be a matter of conjecture without definitive or only partial evidence to support it.

Having already determined that the XIIII Legion would be the central core of the campaign force, as they were already based in vexillation forts along the border of *Ordovician* lands and must have had an excellent idea of the lay of the land with incursions and probable skirmishes with the tribesmen. It therefore follows that by constructing a legionary fortress at Viroconium he could pull the Legion into the fortress and have Auxiliary troops moved up to occupy the vacated vexillation forts in order to start building up his resources in material and livestock from the south east via Watling Street.

Map of Proposed Marching Route(s) of Paulinus and his troops

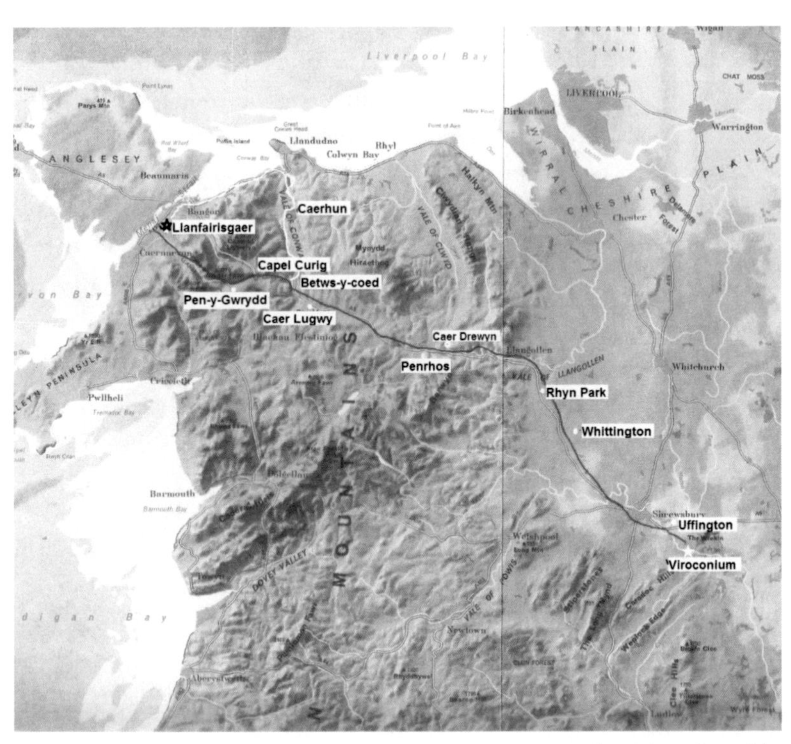

Readers Digest Copyright

Key:

Red Line: the proposed main route

Orange line: the direct route but more diifficult terrain (what is now the A5)

White line: the longest route and probably least effective in engaging the 'enemy'

O: identified marching camps

Note: *The route into western Britannia proposed here is the most viable one based on a land operation (there is no record of Roman naval involvement in the transportation of troops and equipment). It utilises the best route through the mountains from the Roman base at Viroconium via Rhyn Park.*

There are references that suggest that the attack also came from Deva but there is no evidence to suggest that a sizeable force was based here at this time. The first auxiliary fort was not established until around 74 AD. Paulinus may well have dispatched a couple of cohorts of auxiliaries and veterans to ensure that the Deceangli did not join in the fray against him.

As to which route they took down on to the lowlands opposite Mona (Anglesey), these will be discussed later.

As a military campaign it would have been prudent to build up the military force as close to the 'entry point' into 'hostile' territory as possible but in a good defensive position. Rhyn Park near Chirk in Shropshire (and close to the Llangollen Pass into mid Wales) has been identified as a large fort/marching camp that would have been used during the mid 1st Century AD period quite probably by Ostorius Scapula and Didius Gallus. It was of a large enough scale (it is a plateau area which easily accommodated the 17 ha fort, which could temporarily 'house' a force of about 10.000 men and animals [based on accepted figures of 480-690 soldiers per hectare]. This fort is only approximately 28 miles from Viroconium alongside which runs the river Severn and river Perry. There is also evidence of Roman marching camps en route at Uffington and Whittington which may have been constructed/reused specifically for this campaign.

The proposed route from Rhyn Park outlined on the

map is based purely on many hours pouring over OS maps of the region and identifying the most expedient routes to their goal. Using accepted Roman troop marching days and distances, the presence of sizeable water courses and wide good firm valley floors (which may well have been ancient track ways by the time the Romans came to use them and which may be why centuries later, road builders created the main A5 highway to the Isle of Anglesey). Field work was undertaken by the author to follow these proposed likely routes (given the parameters the campaign march would have required, from Viroconium north and west through the valleys of the Welsh mountains to the shore of the Menai Strait facing Mona) to confirm the viability of the premise. Referring to the map overleaf, the proposed route goes from Rhyn Park through to Capel Curig to routes via the Llanberis or Nant Ffrancon Passes. There is the possibility that they could have travelled along the Conwy Valley from Betws-y-coed, attacked and destroyed the *Deceangli* tribal centre at Caerhun (though there is no record of such events occuring) and then moved on to the coast and followed it west to the Menai Strait.

The concensus amongst historians and in the classical texts is that the Roman soldiers marching day was from 7.00 am to 3.00 pm and between 14 and 20 miles per day dependant on terrain and weather conditions.

As has already been established, there were no permanent Roman forts deep in this territory at that time. However, Roman troops did follow a set pattern when on campaign - which would have left a 'footprint' of their presence (though over the millennia many of them would have been lost to erosion or farming techniques). At the end of each marching day the Roman troops would establish a temporary camp for the night (why and how will be covered later).

Possible Routes: Approximate Marching Distances
(to nearest mile)

Rhyn Park → Capel Curig → Llanberis Pass→ Menai Strait * = 65 miles+
At an av. 17 miles per day = 4 day march ^

Rhyn Park→ Capel Curig → Nant Ffrancon Pass → Menai Strait* = 66 miles+
At an av. 17 miles per day = 4 day march ^

Rhyn Park → Betws-y-coed → Conwy Valley → Coast → Menai Strait* = 78 miles+
At an av. 17 miles per day = 5 day march ^

* Llanfair-is-gaer parish, close to the Menai Strait (*after carefully reviewing a topographical map ot the area it appears to be the most probable site for his camp, near to one of the narrowest parts of the Strait*).
+ These figures were obtained by using a route mapping system based on current road networks. The actual distances may have been shorter as they may well have followed a more direct route along the valley floors, though obstacles along the way may have made them deviate somewhat, i.e. swollen rivers, rock falls.
^ This can only be used as an approximation, difficult terrain, they may have been required to bridge rivers where fords where not available, any military action they may have taken would all have slowed the daily march of the column up.

Campaign marching camps/forts were meant to be only temporary, as a defensive camp at the end of a days march, so there were no substantial stone walls or buildings. However, they did have a distinctive ditch and rampart particular to Roman construction. In areas where erosion, farming practices or other human activities have had little impact on the landscape remains of these structures still exist today. Discovery and evidence of their existence and positions has been seriously enhanced with the use of aerial surveys and identifying crop marks. The occupation dates of these camps has been reliant on dating material being found within them and even then, there is no guarantee that they were not constructed before or used again after that material was deposited. So attributing them to a specific time period is somewhat difficult

Using data from current OS maps, the remains of temporary marching camps have been archaeologically identified along the proposed route: Uffington just to the NW of Shrewsbury, Whittington to the NE of Oswestry. Penrhos, (just SW of Corwen, Gwynedd), Caer Llugwy near Betws-y-coed and Penygwryd on the NE flank of Yr Wyddfa (Snowdon), at the junction of the passes leading NW to Llanberis pass and SW to Beddgelert. All are adjacent to large watercourses and set up on good defensible positions.

Currently Identified Marching Camps on Route between Viroconium and Menai

Camp	**NG Ref**	**Area ha.**	**Capacity**(**men**)
1. Uffington	SJ5213	16-18	7,680-12,420
2. Whittington	SJ3530	15	7,200-10,350
3. Rhyn Park *	SJ3037	17	8,160-11.730
4. Penrhos	SJ0442	16.8	7,680-11,040
5. Caer Llugwy	SH7457	1.6	768-1,104
6. Penygwryd	SH6655	4	1,920-2,760

** There are 2 forts here, the larger being the earlier one and attributed to Ostorius Scapula, the smaller (5.7-7 ha) and later one to Sextus Julius Frontius AD 75*

Note:

5. Caer Llugwy is more the size of a vexillation camp
6. Penygwryd has been attributed to the Governorship of Frontius or Agricola, as have other such camps in this region when Roman roads were being established as part of Roman 'control' of the region.

No trace of marching camps have been found (to date) along the alternative route from Betws-y-coed via the Nant Ffrancon valley to Bangor, or along the Conwy Valley.

The March

The starting/assembly point for this campaign is not known, so a number of reasoned assumptions have been made. As the XIIII Legion was based at the Legionary fort of Viroconium (Wroxeter) it and associated supporting troops would probably have left with a column of wagons, mules and livestock following the river Severn across the Shropshire plain (passing what is now Shrewsbury), and on to the large marching fort known to have been at Rhyn Park. The earlier fort defence system at Rhyn Park (see photograph overleaf) consisted of a double ditch system, the outer ditch much more substantial then the inner, enclosing an area of around 42 acres (17 ha). The north-western corner-angle has been lost to erosion by the Afon Ceiriog. There are four gateways, all protected by tutulus outworks, those to north and south are centrally placed in their sides, those in the eastern and western defences are off-set towards the north; the fortress would therefore have faced north across the Ceiriog. Interesting in that it suggests that they expected enemy attacks from the north?

The main part of the cavalry would have been at the head of the marching column acting as the vanguard, followed by a long line of the Legion infantry cohorts.

The plateau of Rhyn Park today, facing NW, with the river Ceiriog in the valley behind the tree line in the distance and the Morlas Brook in the valley behind the camera.

Behind them came the army's baggage, servants, carts with grain, heavy supplies of artillery equipment, ammunition, construction materials plus officers furniture. At the rear came the best units of cavalry and infantry to defend against attack from the rear. The lighter units would have been arranged around the formation as scouts and flankers. The vanguard troops would leave at around 7.00am but the rearguard may not actually leave the camp until several hours later after the last of the wheeled vehicles had left, so arriving at the next camp after much of the work had already been done. In more hostile terrain the Romans would have set marching columns in tighter order so that the carts and wagons could be well defended in case of attack.

The Romans called the baggage train the *IMPEDIMENTUM*, from which the word impediment (meaning obstruction) is derived. If not carefully managed the train (consisting of 100 carts or more drawn by mules or oxen and driven by non-combatants) really could impede the march, and a wise commander also had to guard against loss from attack by the enemy.

Clearly what we see in the plains and valleys of Shropshire and Wales today is totally different from what the Romans would have observed, original forest would have been plentiful even if a lot of the southern lands of the *Cornovii* had been cleared for farming. Yet what would have been evident were trackways used by local people in order to move livestock and produce to trade between the various regions of eastern 'Wales' and the lowlands of Shropshire.

For the most part valley floors along the proposed route appear to be easily accessible for a mobile force, though how much natural forest there was in this area, and how different the topography and forestation of the valleys floors was at that time is a matter of debate.

The route the author has chosen lends itself to be the most obvious and logistically correct route that Paulinus's force would have taken as far as Betws-y-coed (based on the tactics I have read about of other successful Roman Generals). It is is only a theory and can be easily challenged... 'why not sail around western Britannia and attack Mona from the sea, or follow the Conwy valley and attack from the east, or march through the Clwydian valley and along the coast?'

Given what information there is to read about the man and the soldier, Paulinus appears to have been an astute tactician. Certainly if the records of his exploits in the Atlas Mountains and how later he dealt with the Boudican revolt. Knowing his 'enemy', utilising his experience and the collection of key tactical information from previous engagements and campaigns in the Welsh mountains. Being decisive in his planning and effective in its execution was his order of the day. The key to any armies success was food and fresh water. The proposed route (though based on today's levels) gives the greatest access to his large marching army, though the other routes offerd up are good tactically the water supply is not sufficeint for such a large force to drink everyday.

Much of this route follows the roadway we know today as the A5 (constructed in between 1813 and 1826). It would seem that trackways could well have been in use for centuries or at least a major part of the route to Betws-y-coed. In an article by David Ackerly on *'Thomas Telford: The Road to Holyhead'*, David states that in 1808 Telford was given the task of reporting on the road between Shrewsbury and Holyhead. After considering various alternative routes through the Tanat and Ceiriog valleys he settled on what is now the A5. Prior to this, the route from Betws-y-coed to Bangor followed the Afon Conwy valley and the coast of the Menai Strait, a long and 'tortuous' route. Apparently the only difficult section was just west of Llangollen, between the Berwyn Mountain and Glyndyfrdwy, where a significant amount of blasting needed to be done to create a relatively low incline roadway.

The only known contemporary hill fort along the pass is Caer Drewyn, with large stone ramparts situated just to the north of the river Dee and to the east of Corwen.

The other key factor is the historical presence of the armies marching camps. Roman had standardised the construction of their temporary, by organising a defensive camp it could protect it marching army from sneak attacks and the troops, horses would have been well fed and rested for the following days march or battle.

The Roman Marching Camp

The most detailed surviving description of a Roman military fort/marching camp, a **castra** (a small fort of 500 men was known as a castellum) is in the *De Munitionibus Castrorum* (translated as *'Concerning the fortifications of a military camp'*) believed to date from between the late 1st to early 2nd century AD. It was attributed to Hyginus Gromaticus but more likely to have been by an unknown author. It states that *'the first choice of a site should be one which rises gently above the plain, on a distinctive rise and the porta documana is set at the highest point so that the area is dominated by the camp. The porta praetoria should always face the enemy. The second on a plain, the third on a hill, the fourth on a mountain. The fifth choice of anywhere necessary is the unavoidable camp'*.

The process of establishing a marching-camp would start when the general in command of an army determined the proposed area where the day's march would terminate. A detail of officers (a military tribune and several centurions), known as the mensores ('measurers') led by the by the Praefectus castorum (Camp Prefect), would be charged with surveying the area and determining the best location for the praetorium (the commander's tent). A standard would then be planted to mark the spot and gromatici (land surveyors) who used a groma sighting device consisting of a vertical staff with horizontal cross pieces and vertical plumb-lines). Ideally the process started in the centre of the planned camp at the site of the headquarters tent or building (principia where the praetorium would be situated). 'Streets' (the Via Praetoria and Via Principalis) and other features were marked with coloured pennants or rods. Measured from this spot, a perimeter would be marked out with 4 gates, many camps in Britannia have been found to be longer than they are wide (in permanent forts the number of gates may well have exceeded 4.

The size of the camp would be determined by the size of the force that would be contained within it (as stated earlier, the accepted figure is between 480 and 690 soldiers per ha.). Along the perimeter, a ditch (fosse) would be excavated (minimum width of 5 Roman Feet, 3 RF deep) and the spoil used to build an earthen rampart (agger) 8 ½ RF wide and 6 RF high. On top of this rampart a palisade (vallum) of cross-hatched or upright wooden stakes with sharpened points (pila muralia/ sudes/vallis) was erected.

A representation of a Sudis Pallisade. (Wikimedia Commons)

The fort was playing card in shape. Within the ramparts, a standard, elaborate plan was to allocate space in a pre-set pattern for the tents of each of the various components of the campaign force: officers, legionary infantry and cavalry, auxiliary infantry and cavalry.

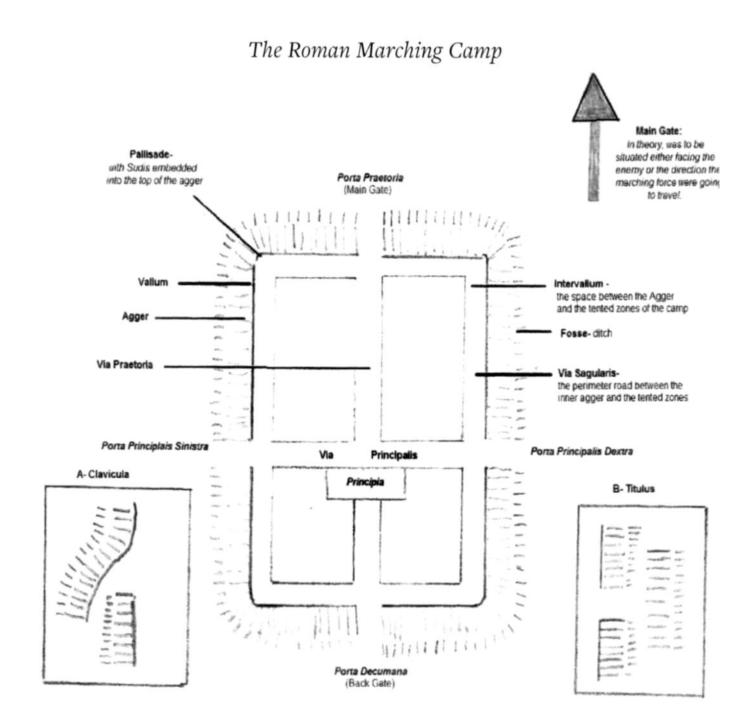

Sketch showing the basic set up of a Roman Marching Fort

Vallum: a defensive system comprising of a ditch (*fosse*), and bank (*agger*) constructed of the and earth excavated from the ditch, mounted by a pallisade of shaped upright wooden stakes (*sudis*)
Intervallum: this is the gap between the vallum and the tent lines within the fort. It is also allowed the soldiers unhindered access to the ascensi (*turf steps*) built in the inner vallum and up to the pallisade in the event of an attack. It also attacked as a 'safety zone' inside the fort so that burning missiles coming over the vallum would hopefully fall short and reduce the risk of the tents etc of catching fire.
Principea: the tent and headquarters of the Legate/Campaign commander
Porta: the number of gates was dependent on the size of the force housed within it. Normaly 4, there could be as many as six, the extra gates would be situated on the dextra and sinistra sides of the fort.
Extra External Defences
A – Clavicula: an extension of the vallum in front of the porta forming a defendable passageway and a 'permitted' access to the camp by the enemy but forcing the enemies unsheilded sworn arm be exposed to the defenders on the pallisade.
B – Titulus: a short length of a vallum either straight or curved outwards in front of the porta.
These would be likely to be situated at the dextra and sinistra gates, leaving the Main and Back gates clear.

The idea of the standardising of camps and forts was so that the man and unit would know exactly in which section of the camp to pitch his/their tents and corral its animals. Each soldier would also know exactly what his role in the construction process would be, equipped with picks and shovels for the purpose. The construction of a marching-camp would take an army just a couple of hours (weather dependant of course), a valuable tactic for speedy construction in hostile territory.

In reality the camps needed to be situated on the most suitable ground: i.e. preferably level, dry, clear of trees and rocks, a good defensible position and close to large sources of drinkable water. The ability to forage and get access to good grazing for horses and the mules also had to be taken into consideration.

The standard measurements for a marching camp were a minimum size ditch width of 5 feet and a depth of 3 feet, whilst the rampart should be 8 feet wide and six feet high (whether the sudis pallisade was also included in this is not stated). Which makes it a distinct structure on the landscape such that it could be still visible for centuries.

Note: In Roman period 1 foot = 11.654 inches or 296 mm

The advantages of fortified marching-camps were therefore substantial. Properly patrolled (1 cohort would normally be sufficient to protecting the camp overnight) and fortified, these marching camps made surprise attacks impossible and successful attacks rare – in fact, there is no case recorded in the ancient literature of a Roman marching-camp being successfully stormed. The level of security afforded by these fortified camps allowed the soldiers to sleep soundly, while animals, baggage and supplies were safely corralled within its boundaries. The camp layout was organised so that the cavalry could respond quickly and the troops could man the walls quickly If the army engaged an enemy near a marching-camp, a small garrison of a few hundred men would be more than able to defend the camp and its contents.

To give an idea of the size of some of these forts please see the list on page 128 of the 'Currently Identified Marching Camps on Route between Viroconium and the Menai Strait Route'.

In contrast to this, the Celtic war bands slept where they could and appear not to have been effectively organised enough to construct a fortified encampment to protect themselves reliant probably on sentries and therefore making them extremely vulnerable to surprise attacks.

Bwlch y Ddeufaen

The Marching Route Options

The following proposed marching routes are based on a number of important points. Given that this operation by Paulinus was to finally subdue the tribes and Druids based in this region the Romans needed to strike through the lands of the Ordovices with an overwhelming force and break the resistance here before they reached the Strait and Mona.

What needed to be considered (based on the information they had from many different sources some maybe more reliable than others) were the most viable military routes they could take to be most effective in reaching their targets effectively with minimum impediments in regard to difficult terrain for such a great force of men and baggage trains. Roman marching camps that have been clearly archaeologically identified in the region have played a part in the proposed routes along with the generally agreed daily marching distances for Roman troops on campaign (with a baggage train) and looking at their access to ample water sources and within the 300m distance – water courses are not likely to have changed significantly over the millenia in these valleys. The elevation has been included as an approximate guide to the ease or difficulty of achieving average daily marching distance for the whole column; troops/cavalry on their own may well have travelled much further in a day.

Phase 1

- **Viroconium** to **Rhyn Park** -
  Distance: approx 28 miles
  Elevation: Rise over 230' from start to finish

This is longer than a standard daily march for legions and all there equipment. In this scenario it is more likely that staging marching camps at Uffington and Whittington where used to build up his campaign force on 'friendly' ground and then pull the full force together at Rhyn Park.

On-route water sources: river Severn, river Perry, Afon Ceiriog at Rhyn

- **Rhyn Park** to **Penrhos** (near Druid)
  Distance: approx 20 miles
  Elevation: river valley rise over 358' from start to finish
  Penrhos was a large camp occupying the summit of a rounded hill overlooking the confluence of the Afon Alwyn with the Afon Dyfrdwy.

  On-route water sources: river Dee

- **Penrhos** to **Caer Llugwy**# (between Betws-y-coed and Capel Curig)
  Distance: approx 23 miles*
  Elevation: rise/fall/rise over 780' from start to finish

Caer Llugwy is also known as Bryn-y-Gefeiliau, and is situated in a loop of the Afon Llugwy. The camps construction has been dated to around AD 90 and was one of a series of vexillation forts (housing some 500 men) constructed during this period.

* As the terrain here is becoming increasing more demanding especially for carts and oxen, the distance travelled is likely to have been much less than 20 miles a day.

If this marching route is correct it suggests that there may be a 'lost' marching camp, possibly somewhere between Pentrefoelas (approx 12 miles from Penrhos) and Betws-y-coed (approx 19 miles from Penrhos).

On-route water sources: Afon Alwen, Afon Ceirw and the river Conwy.

Note: # indicates the current names used purely for the purpose of points of reference along the proposed marching routes, there are no clear records of settlements at these points during this period.

- **Penrhos** to **Betws-y-coed**
  Distance: approx 19 miles
  Elevation: gradual rise and fall of approx. 820' from start to finish.

  On-route water sources: Afon Merddwr and Afon Conwy

There would have been little risk to this huge force travelling from Viroconium to Rhyn Park and the Romans had a clear 'understanding' with the local tribes. From Rhyn Park through the Dee valley past what is now Llangollen and up to Penrhos and Betws-y-coed the advancing army would have been clearly visable to the local inhabitants in the hills. There is no mention of 'guerilla' attacks on the column by local tribes or open battle, it is more than possible that any local fighters would have retreated closer to the heartland of Snowdonia hoping to meet up with more local fighters as there were no recorded large fortified enclosures or hill forts on the route that could have acted as a defensive barrier.

Betws-y-coed is the first axis point for a possible alternate onward campaign route:

Phase 2

Route 1: From Betws-y-coed, North along the wide river Conwy Valley to Conwy# then follow the coastline West to Llanfair-is-gaer # on the Menai Strait

Distance: approx.36 miles and tidal dependant
(16 miles to Conwy and 20 miles to Llanfa-is-gaer#).
Elevation: relatively flat +

On-route water sources: Afon Conwy as far as Conwy. From Conwy to Bangor they would have only crossed 3 watercourses: Afon Ddu, Afon Rhaeadr-fawr and Afon Ogwen (all of which run south to north into the Irish Sea).

There are known settlements of the period along this route in the Conwy Valley so there is a possibility there may have been at least skirmishes with local tribesmen (*Ordovician or Deceangli*), but there are no classical records of any such events in regard to this campaign. Beyond these they could have marched relatively easily west along the coast to the Llanfair-is-gaer near the Menai Strait between Bangor# and Caernarfon#. There are a number of contemporary tribal settlements along this coastline and on the overlooking hills of Snowdonia. There are no recorded archaeological remains or crop/parch marks of a marching fort along this whole route dating from this time period – it is possible that any evidence may have been lost to erosion or farming practices over the millenia.

Note: From Conwy# the troops would have had to march along the shoreline (movement dictated by the tides) for a number of miles because of the hill promontories at Penmaenbach and Penmaenmawr blocking any direct land based march. If this axis point alternative route was ignored for a more direct route, the march would have continued from Betws-y-coed# to Capel Curig# for routes through the mountains of Snowdonia.

OR From Betws-y-coed to Capel Curig

Distance: approx 5 miles
Elevation: gradual rise of 577' from start to finish
On-route water source: Afon Llugwy
See Elevation Profiles of the Possible Marching Routes

Capel Curig: second axis point for alternate onward campaign routes:

Route 2: Capel Curig#. South westerly along the valley to Penygwryd* and up through Pen-y-Pass, down though the Llanberis Pass and across lowland to Llanfair-is-gaer#

Distance: approx. 18 miles
Elevation: See Elevation Profiles of Possible Marching Routes

On-route water sources: Nant Gwryd, Afon Nant Peris, Llyn Peris, Llyn Padarn and Afon Rhythallt.

Note: there is a very steep incline up the river valley between Glyder Fawr and Yr Wyddfa (Snowdon) up to Pen -y-Pass and into the Llanberis Pass and would not have been a viable route for an army with wagons.

* Penygwryd: The remains of a legionary-sized camp was strategically located at the head of the Dyffryn Mymbr and the junction of the passes leading north-west to Llanberis, south-west to Beddgelert and east to Capel Curig, Its construction has been attributed to either Governors Frontius or Agricola.

Route 3: Capel Curig#, via the Nant Ffancon Pass to Bethesda#, Tregarth# , on to Llanfair-is-gaer# at the Menai Strait.

Distance: approx. 18 miles
Elevation: See Elevation Profiles of Possible Marching Routes
On-route water source: Afon Llugwy, Llyn Ogwen and Afon Ogwen

Note: there is a 'choke point' at the western end of Lyn Ogwen but it is passable.

Routes 2 and 3 both have their merits and disadvantages with regard to terrain and there would have been little in food to forage in these mountain passes but both would take them to the lowlands opposite Mona directly in the shortest space of time.

There is potentially a fourth route the Romans could have taken. Leaving Capel Curig south eastwards along the southern flank of Yr Wyddfa to Beddgelert and then follow the valley north west via Rhyd-ddu (where there is a 'choke point' the valley is very narrow here), Betws Garmon, Caethro and to Caernarfon. Water sources would have followed these valleys but it is the longest route at approximately 28 miles and would having extended their marching day by at least 24 hrs. There are no indications of marching camps in this area dating to this period.

Studying all the military logistics required for this sizeable army travelling on nothing more than trackways the route that appears most viable is Route 2 – which today exists as the A5.

Seutonius Paulinus's Grand Plan would have been the total crushing of the resistance that he believed was being fuelled from the home of the Druid's, Mona. In order to achieve this Grand Plan he had to have had a grand strategy and to do this he would have drawn on his own training and experiences of his commanders. He would also have given careful consideration to where they fought their battles.

Though fully trained and with comrades who may well have fought in many battles, the Roman soldier's state of mind (as is the case with any soldier throughout history) was critical to military success. The commander must create an environment to positively nurture the soldiers psyche as it could directly impact on the outcome of the battle or campaign.

Numerous factors could influence the soldier's effectiveness:

- Weather and climate
- Exhaustion
- Lack of sleep
- Accessibility to food and water
- Marching long distances (especially in a difficult terrain)
- Crossing waterways (in full armour especially in the face of the enemy).

The Roman army was so successful because it had learnt from each new enemy it faced, whether it was new weapons (e.g. the Gladius was based on a Greek weapon) effective tactical formations (e,g. the manciple formation adopted after the Samnite Wars) or very mobile troops (light cavalry used by the Thracians in their war against Rome). By incorporating what they saw as enhancing their own military capability, they believed they could defeat anyone who challenged them; as long as they were led by a good military commander!

One of the key elements of a Roman soldier's training was to fear the disciplinary punishments he would face from his officers and comrades more than anything else, including the enemy. In most situations this was all that was required but the commander, if he was to be truly successful, had to factor in as many elements in his

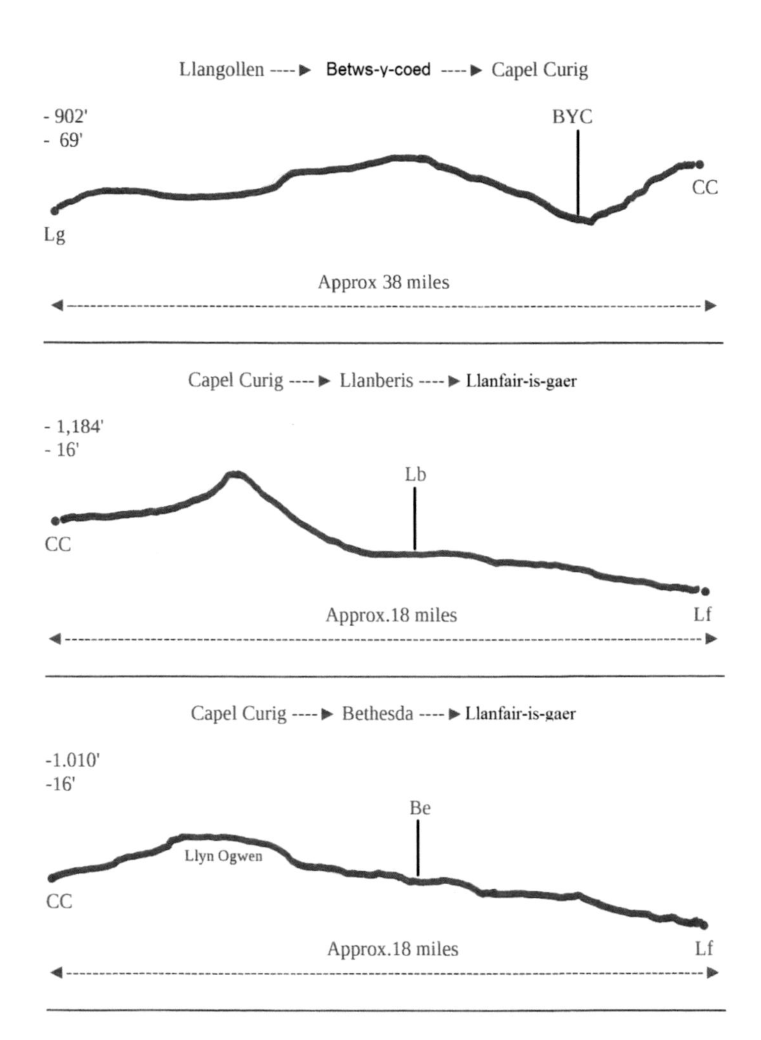

Elevation Profiles of the Possible Marching Routes

planning to minimise the above factors.

Paulinus clearly got his forces through the mountains of western Britannia, where weather would have been a factor: rain storms can quickly roll in. Exhaustion, lack of sleep and marching long distances were unlikely to have been much in evidence as the force was seemingly not under pressure in a forced march or harassment by the 'enemy'. Food would have been carried with them and there would have been an ample supply of fresh water in the rivers they travelled along on route.

Segontium

The mainland settlements opposite Mona

Across the Strait on the mainland lay the tribal lands of the *Gangani*, the *Ordovices (the 'hammer' people)* and the *Deceangli*. [Please refer to the diagram 'The Lands of the Tribes of Western Britannia AD 40' page 45]

To the West lies the Llŷn Peninsula, land ascribed to the *Gangani* tribe. The only visible major settlement today is Tre'r Ceiri hill fort, standing at 450 m above sea level on the exposed peak of Yr Eifl. Finds have revealed that its initial construction was circa 200 BC and developed into a site with around 20 round houses, stone walls and turf roofs. During the 1st century AD it was expanded further to 150 houses and the fort walls up to 4 m high (which are largely still intact). Further archaeological digs found pottery, iron tools, stone spindle-whorls and glass beads, belonging to the Romano-Brythonic period (AD 50-400), thus showing that it continued as a settlement during the occupation of this region we now know by the Roman army.

The *Gangani* were a Celtic people who are believed to have originally migrated to southern Ireland (Ptolomy identifies such a group in the area now known as Leinster) so were a sea travelling tribe. It is more than possible that a section of the tribe may have migrated again to North Wales; some onto the Llŷn Peninsula. It is believed a larger splinter group of this tribe (the *Deceangli*) went further east and settled in hill forts on the Clwydian hills (this area of the region was rich in Copper and Lead) with their tribal centre believed to be at Canovium.

It is quite possible that it may have been a 'confederacy' of extended family units, all with the same goal of farming the land the best way they could. They would have been spread out over a wide area as good farm land would have been limited in the mountains and valleys especially if the land was already inhabited by indigenous peoples. Ptolomy could quite well have been recording the 'main' tribes that the Romans had been dealing with and have had 'no knowledge' of these sub-groups.

There is no clear evidence as is how the *Ordovices*' settled the land between these two groups, will be seen later; the *Ordovices* it would appear, were a more warlike tribe than either of them. The *Ordovices* did have a strong presence in the land opposite the island, with 'forts' and settlements throughout the area and down the Lanberis Pass, many of which are still visible today e.g. Dinas Dinorwig *(fort of the Ordovices)* which has an internal area of some 1.2 ha, and is sited on the north eastern ridge of the valley above the Afon Seiont where the pass opens out onto the plain facing Ynys Môn.

What is certainly clear from all the map records is that there were no large settlements here. They were all relatively small (up to 100 individuals), probably extended family units living in a 'homestead' (*Welsh: Tre*[1]). The hills would not have supported large groups of people and they would have been spread thinly. Larger family units would have been located on the valley floors in areas where it was possible to farm. The hill fort construction seems to be a reaction to raids initially and were for protection only.

Note: there are a few historical references to a tribe called the Segontii who were implied to have lived in this area, or that Segontium (Caernarfon) was named after them, but no reliable texts have been identified to confirm this. In Old Welsh it is called Caer Seiont 'fort on the Seiont river'. A Roman fort was not established here until AD 77.

Given that the population is apparently spread out and

---

[1] Tre (f) = a homestead and later, a small settlement or village // 100 Tref = a Cantref

the hill forts[2] are not large it would be fair to presume that trying to bring a 'warrior' force together in response to a large attacking force would have been extremely difficult to do, especially if there was no charismatic chieftain to lead them. Their only real advantage was that they knew their lands well and could use guerrilla methods effectively with a small force of mobile warriors, using the 'hit and run' tactics.

Whichever route this huge Roman Campaign force took, it would have clearly given notice to *the Ordovician* tribesmen along the way they were travelling that the size of the force showed that the Romans meant business.

Archaeological evidence shows that there were lots of small settlements and hill forts (e.g. Dinas Dinorwig – 'Fort of the Ordovices') in the valleys, foothills and mountains on route between Snowdonia and the Strait (ref diagram on page 151: Dinas Tŷ-Du, Caer near Glasgoed, an enclosure near Cae-coch, hut enclosure near Caermynydd, Caer Carreg-y-frân, Castell Gron). There was also Dinas (fort) on the Strait. There may well have been more settlements in this region but any remains have been lost in time. There was also the *Gangani* tribe to the west in a large hillfort (*Tre'r Ceiri*) of which there is no mention of in this conflict

---

[2] *The term 'hill fort' is probably not the correct term to use for these structures.The term 'hill fort' encompasses simple enclosures up to forts of 6 ha or more. Those less than 0.5 ha could be classed as fortified 'homesteads'. Structures between 1 and 6 ha as pens for livestock, farmers 'markets' for livestock and crops, temporary refuges in the event of unrest in the area or stongholds for local cheiftains. Those of 6 ha and more would have been probably for the protection of a substantial number of people. Interestingly north of the line drawn between Barmouth and Chester there are of those currently identified 8 over 6 ha, 20 between 1 and 6 ha and 46 less than 1 ha (3, 1 and 5 respectively on Ynys Môn). Certainly evidence from the archaeological work done by Professor Barry Cunliffe and others on the Iron Age forts has shown that very few were what you would call garrison forts.*

with Paulinus' troops. In truth we do not know what size of 'force' was facing Paulinus and whether they were indeed hardened warriors or just farmers.

Given that these occupied areas were faced with such a large force of well trained and armed troops what would the inhabitants have done? Remain in their strongholds and not venture out, fight, surrender or flee by whatever means possible to Mona believing it to be a safe haven from these 'invaders'.

As a fighting force about to attack what they believed to be the centre of resistance to their authority over the lands, they certainly would not have left the rear or the flanks of that force exposed to any possible attack from 'local anti-Roman forces'. They would have made sure that any resistance threat was eliminated or at least neutralised. It was also be expedient militarily to have the camp in a position akin to that of Rhyn Park; an open relatively flat space with good/commanding views over the whole area and near to local water sources. To that end the proposal of the Roman camp being situated near to or at the area we know today as Llanfair-is-gaer is a reasonable suggestion even if there is no archaeological or classical text evidence to support. This area also overlooks the Strait at a point where an invasion crossing would be possible. It is at one of the narrow points of the Strait but here also it has gently sloping land down to the water line and gentle slopes up on the opposite Mona bank making rapid troop manoeuvres much easier to carry out in an offensive against the islands defenders.

Paulinus' Arrival at the Menai Strait

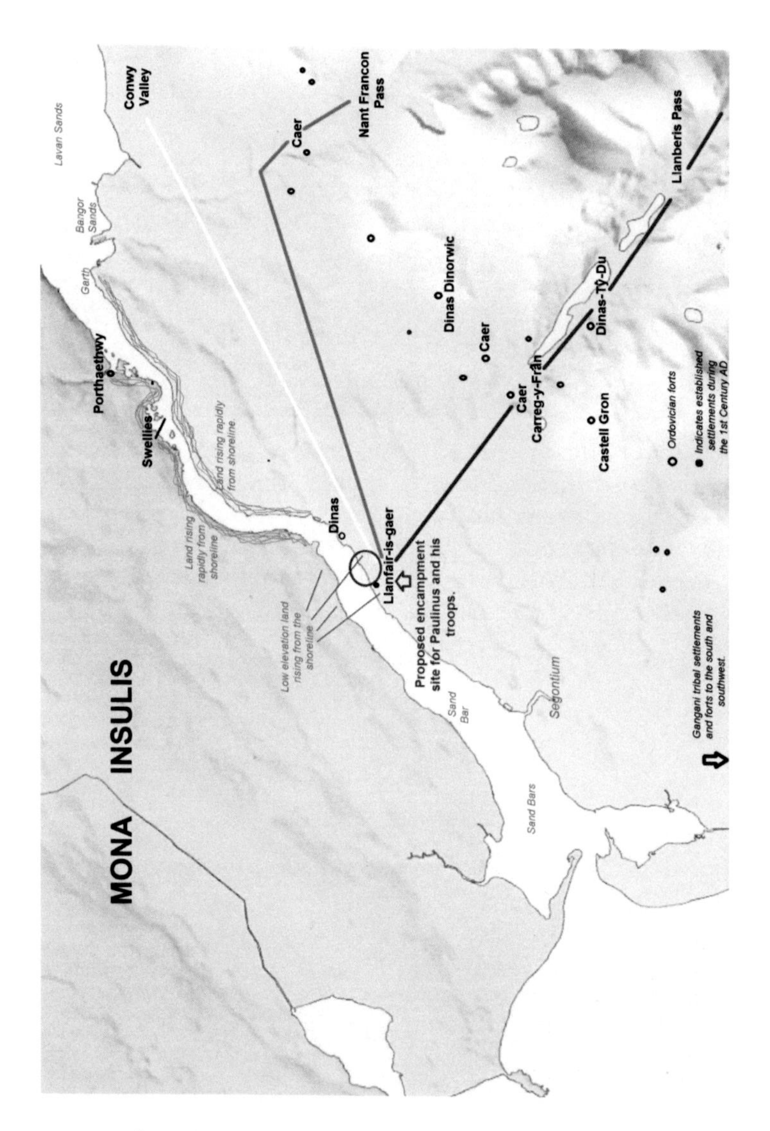

Note: The white, orange and red lines lines indicate the proposed 3 possible routes Paulinus could have taken to reach the shore of the Strait.

View from Barras (Mona) looking out across the Strait at Low Water towards the mainland. It shows the mud/stone/sand Mona shoreline, the exposed sand bar of Traeth Gwyllt in the middle of the channel (which would have made a crossing here impossible). In the back ground is Yr Wyddfa rising high into the clouds with the Nant Ffrancon Pass to its left and the Llanberis Pass to the right.

View from Moel y Don (Mona) at Low Water looking SW down the Strait exposing the firm mud and sand bay where the Romans would have landed safely for their attack, even on a rising tide after crossing from Llanfair-is-gaer.

The Menai Strait

There is nothing in the classical texts that gives any indication as to any events occurring along the marching route, the establishing of their camp beside the Strait and what preparations were made to establish a bridgehead on the island itself. Therefore, in order to try and determine what possible actions took place it will be necessary to look at the problems that faced Paulinus and his troops on the shore of the Strait.

The primary concern was to get his troops across this 'waterway barrier' as an effective fighting force as quickly as possible, with minimal losses and giving his men sufficient covering fire against the enemy.

His forces would be in full view of the enemy he would need to strike effectively and rapidly before the 'enemy' could be reinforced. What he needed now was accurate reconnaissance and intelligence.

Paulinus was faced with a 21 mile stretch of water. He would have quickly ascertained it could not be spanned with a bridge, or with the use of pontoon boat bridge to cross it as the tidal ranges and currents would have discounted both these as impractical.

His next course of action therefore would have been to have the whole length 'mapped out' to determine:-

(a) whether there were crossing/ferry points.
(b) if so were these points practical for his needs as launching sites, together with data on the approximate width of the Strait along its whole length at both high and low tides
(c) the topography of the land on either side (including shorelines and sandbars)

(d) the available natural resources to aid in his campaign i.e. woodland for the construction of boats etc, a good and ample water source, food for his men and forage for his animals.

The shoreline areas of both banks of Mona and the mainland between what we now know Plas Newydd and Beaumaris including the area known as the 'Swellies' (narrowing to around 400 m wide) rise fairly quickly to between 30 and 50m above the Strait with a relatively rocky shoreline (more so between Porthaethwy and Plas Newydd) which militarily is not ideal for the mass landing of troops and cavalry. The uneven ground and slow progress on landing would have made them acutely vulnerable to an attack from the island's defenders.

At the SW approach of the Strait from its mouth at Abermenai Point and Fort Belan up to the Traeth Gwyllt sand bank near Barras, there are large shifting sand bars. It is also here that the Strait reaches some of its widest points; approximately a 1000 m. From the northern most tip of Traeth Gwyllt (approximately 750m wide at mean low water) the Strait begins to narrow up to Moel y Don (about 300m at mean low water) and the land on either side gently slope down to the waters edge to a mostly mud and sand shore, with a wide expanse of sand and stone shoreline (at low water) in a bay to the SW of Moel y Don.

Given that there were 'hostiles' on the Mona bank any mapping of that shore would have been done by careful observation and local knowledge. Good Roman commanders would not have hesitated to exploit useful intelligence. They would have sent out patrols, mounted raids to probe for weaknesses, snatching 'hostiles' and local inhabitants (including any local ferrymen they had found still on the mainland shore) to gain as much relevant information (not necessarily freely given) as they could.

There was also the fact that Caer Idris and Caer Leb - hill fort/settlements – on the island were within 3 km of the Roman held shore.

Having gained a fairly accurate understanding of the shoreline and the gentle slopes beyond, his concern would have been how he could use the tides and currents here to his best advantage. While the boats were being constructed, Paulinus certainly would have had his men make detailed observation of the daily tides and the tidal ranges over a period of weeks, if required. Obviously this event occurred over 1900 years ago so the tides may well have altered in height, and weather conditions may well have been very different from what they are today. In order to get some sense of what he would have had to deal with, a present day maritime tidal data for the Strait (please see chart) which offers some credence to the theory of where the author believe the Romans landed and how they may have used the tides to do it.

The Tides

The world's tides run on a 12 hour cycle twice a day (High, Low, High and Low water levels); one will run it full course during the day and the second through the hours of darkness. In the Strait, a rising tide starts in the SW at Abermenai causing the water in the Strait to flow NE as the water level rises. At the same time the incoming tide is flowing up and around Mona until after a few hours it reaches around the NW end of the Strait and starts to flow in a SW direction towards the Strait. By the time the NE flow tide is beginning to weaken (but is still rising) the tidal flow is now NE to SW (the sequence is in reverse on the ebb tide). Slack water times (the peak of high and low tides) will therefore vary along the length of the Strait; as an indicator, slack water time at the Swellies is around 1 hour before high and low tides. Low water here may fall below 0.5 m but elsewhere the current minimum depth is never less than 2 m. The Strait in effect has a double tide every 12hrs.The tidal range is significant, an average of 5 mtrs between high and low tides. Translated from shoreline to shoreline at Felinheli, the distance between high water and low water is quite marked; from 650 m down to 300 m. Whether they took the Spring and Neap tides into consideration we will never know. So for the Roman General, his decision would fall between a vanguard attack under the cover of darkness with his main force crossing on the low tide during the

Chart of Twice Daily Tidal Levels Measured at Menai Bridge (2017) Against Datum*
(Measured in Metres)

	1st					2nd				
Month	**MHW**	**MLW**	**Diff.**	**HT**	**LT**	**MHW**	**MLW**	**Diff.**	**HT**	**LT**
May	6.7	1.55	5.15	7.57	0.7	6.5	1.53	4.97	7.6	0.64
June	6.65	1.55	5.1	7.45	0.71	6.5	1.58	4.92	7.55	0.77
July	6.58	1.55	5.1	7.54	0.61	6.54	1.6	4.94	7.57	0.75
August	6.78	1.55	5.23	7.59	0.53	6.5	1.66	4.84	7.6	0.7
September	6.53	1.56	4.97	7.36	0.57	6.62	1.6	5.02	7.53	0.72
October	6.47	1.56	4.91	7.64	0.61	6.68	1.73	4.95	7.72	0.75
November	6.55	1.56	4.99	7.6	0.65	6.67	1.6	5.07	7.64	0.77
December	6.53	1.56	4.97	7.56	0.75	6.67	1.56	5.11	7.49	0.78

Datum = Lowest Astronomical Tides (LAT) which can be predicted to occur under average meteorological conditions and under any combination of astronomical conditions (United Kingdom Hydrographic Office)

MHW: Mean High Water — HT: Highest Tide
MLW: Mean Low Water — LT: Lowest Tide

Spring Tides occur twice a month during the Full moon
Neap tides are especially weak tides which occur during the ¼ moon 7 days after the spring tides.

following day, or his force going across in waves during the day on the low tide under the cover of his ballista fire. Whichever he choose, he had to ensure that the men he sent across spent as little time on the water in full armour and were not exhausted from paddling or rowing across an expanse of water, fighting a current that could be taking them well away from their designated landing area. The the tidal range chart overleaf (for the year 2017) measured at Menai Bridge during the 'Roman summer campaign' months (mid May to mid August) when Paulinus would have made his move against Mona. Also included are the months up to December to give a relative indication of the ranges – information that a certain Roman officer (Agricola) who was present with Paulinus's force may have used to his advantage over a decade later. Using this example as to what the Romans may have observed, it can be used to determine when the boats would have been launched to give them the best possible chance of success.

So for the Roman General, his decision would fall between a vanguard attack under the cover of darkness with his main force crossing on the low tide during the following day, or his force going across in waves during the day on the low tide under the cover of his ballista projectiles. Whichever he chose, he had to ensure that the men he sent across spent as little time on the water in full armour and were not exhausted from paddling or rowing across an expanse of water, fighting a current that could be taking them well away from their designated landing area. The chart above shows the tidal range (for the year 2017) measured at Menai Bridge during the 'Roman summer campaign' months (mid May to mid August) when Paulinus would have made his move against Mona Also included are the months up to December to give a relative indication of the ranges – information that a certain Roman officer (Agricola) who was present with Paulinus's force may have used to his advantage over a decade later. This example of actual recodings give an indication of the tidal levels along the Strait and may have been similar at the time the Romans stood on the mainland bank looking over to Mona. Such recordings would certainly coululd have been used to determine when the boats would have been launched to give them the best possible chance of success.

How different the tidal level ranges were in the 1st Century AD here, which may have had an impact on the crossing distances at both high and low tides. To get some insight into this from researched sea level data there appears to have been little change in global levels between AD 0 and AD 1880[1] however there is strong evidence to suggest that sea level gradually rose in the 20th century and much faster in 21st century – thermal expansion of the oceans and the loss of land based ice due to increased melting:

- Between 1880 and 2009 there was an ocean rise of 210mm[2]
- During the 19th century sea levels rose by 600mm[3] *
- During the 20th century they had risen by 1900 mm[3] *

  (evidenced by geological observations, instrumental records and observed rates).

For the purpose of this proposed theory the author has used recent tidal data as it is more important to determine how and where the Romans could have crossed rather than a matter of ten's of metres extra or less they would have had to row or sail.

---

[1] *Cronin T M (2012) Invited Review: Rapid Sea Level Rise: Quartenary Science Reviews 56 : 11 - 30*

[2] *Church, John A; White. Neil J (2011) 'Sea-level Rise from late 19thCentury to early 20thCentury, Surveys in Geophysics 32 (4-5)*

[3] *Jevrejeva, Svetlana; Moore JC; Grinsted A; Woodworth PL (2008) 'Recent global sea level acceleration started over 200 years ago? Geophysical Research letters.35 (8)*

In order for his troops to spend as little time exposed crossing the Strait, Paulinus would have needed to time his troops landing as near to and just after the low tide (as long as it was onto firm beaches) and advance as quickly as possible up to the High water level mark in order to establish their beachhead.

Chart Representing the Tidal Flow for the Menai Strait between Fort Belan and Felinheli*

	SW Belan	Caernarvon	*Tan-y-Foel* *Llanfair-is-gaer*	*Moel-y-don*	**NE** Port Dinorwic
-6		<1.5 kn			▶
-5	< 3.5 kn ▶		< 1.5 kn		▶
-4		>3.5 kn			▶
-3	>3.5 kn ▶		<3.5 kn		▶
-2	<1.5 kn ▶		< 0.5 kn		▶ Slack Water
-1	◀ <1.5 kn	◀	< 0.5 kn		
HW	◀ >3.5 kn	◀	< 3.5 kn		
+1	◀ >3.5 kn	◀	L<3.5 kn		
+2	◀	< 3.5 kn			
+3	◀	<3.5 kn			
+4	◀	< 0.5 kn			
+5	— — — S l a c k	— — W a t e r	— — —		
+6	<0.5 kn ▶		<1.5 kn		▶

1 knot (kn) ≈ 0.5m/sec **▶ = direction of flow**

* Based on recent (2017) data from UK Hydrographic Office

Notes:

(a) The tidal ranges between Caernarfon and Felinheli are:
High Water: 4.6 - 4.8 m Low Water: 2.1 – 2.4 m

(b) The double tide (from the SW and then the NE) that occurs in the Strait means that High Water and Slack Water do not coincide.

Given these present day recordings of the ebb and flow of the tides (including average current speed) of the area, it is reasonable to propose that the tidal processes (not levels) would have not altered much through the millenia and that the point at which the Romans would have crossed was somewhere between Caernarfon and Felinheli. The data above gives an indication of the times when the tide is running at its fastest, the direction of the dominant current and when the slack tide occurs. The tidal flow along this section would determine the optimum time for the Roman boats containing the infantry with the cavalry horses and their riders swimming alongside (as support for the infantry) to commence the crossing.

From the above chart it appears that the optimum time period for the crossing is 2 hrs before low tide when the current would have been less than 1.5 knots (flowing SW) and no more than 2 hrs after the slack water when the currents pace would be increasing to 3.5 knots in a NW direction. The water levels would be falling to the lowest point meaning that the distance required to travel across the water was at its least.

Abermenai

The Invasion AD 60

The planning would have had to have been meticulous for the attack to be successful, needing elite troops landing, and being able to hold and even expand the bridgehead to allow for more troops to be brought across. Therefore, to ensure that he could achieve this bridgehead he had to get a significant and effective force across the Strait as quickly as possible. In order to do this there were two key elements aside from tides and weather. Firstly he had to have sufficient boats to transport his troops acroos the tidal waterway and an effective strategy to endure that the first wave of troops landed with plenty of covering support to build and maintain a bridgehead to allow more troops to come across and force the 'enemy' back from the beach.

Overleaf is a photograph of Mona's shoreline today approximately 1.5 kms SW of Moel y Don (on the right in the background is Llanfair-is-gaer and beyond that the mountains of Snowdonia). Here it is a pebble and sand beach at low tide on which the Roman troops may well have landed on. The actual water channel is far over to the right along the mainland side of the Strait adjacent to Llanfair-is-gaer.

There are no records of how they got across the Strait but it is possible that the XIIII Legion did bring with it knowledge and expertise from their actions against the Germanic tribes when having to cross the river Rhine from their base at Mogontiacum (Mainz), the Romans favoured bridges but first they had to cross these large rivers in order to secure the opposite bank before contruction of a bridge could commence.

Tacitus does give us some idea of what occurred at this point in his:

Annales Book XIV, Cornelius Tacitus xxix

'...*he* [Governor Gaius Seutonius Paulinus] *therefore*

prepared to attack the island of Mona which had a powerful population and was a refuge for fugitives. He built flat-bottomed vessels to cope with the shallows, and uncertain of the depths of the sea. Thus the infantry crossed, while the cavalry followed by fording or, where the water was deep, swam by the side of their horses.

This could be either the building a considerable number of small boats or much larger flat bottomed boats holding at least a centuria – a century (10 contubernium - 80 men plus a centurion) for the initial landings followed by supplies and replacements until the tide forced them to halt further sailings until the next appropriate tide. Though we do not have much idea as to the size of these flat bottomed boats there are a number of Roman built examples found in archaeological digs around Europe (see overleaf) which are contemporary to this period and which may have been similar to those constructed and used at the Strait. The key was flat bottomed boats; they could be beached easily, refloated on the next tide (especially if the proposed landing site on Mona is correct) and stable enough to have had scorpio mounted on its deck as added protection.

How long it took construct the boats for the assault is not recorded but it will have been in full view of the islanders, they will have known what was coming!

We do not know in what month the attack actually took place and the little data we do have on the action are only short descriptions from classical texts. The only significant reference there is that can give us some indication is Paulinus and his troops rushing back from Mona 'mid-summer' in reaction to the Boudican revolt. These were written many years after the event by Roman historians and others, but lack detail.... though there is some insight into what possibly occurred.

The photographs on the following two pages are the current shorelines where the proposed crossing took place both shores currently have firm ground which would have been ideal for landing boats and armour laden troops.

Proposed embarkation from Llanfair-is-gaer to Barras/Moel y Don: Low Tide

Proposed landing beach between Barras and Moel y Don: Low Tide

Proposed embarkation point from Felinheli to Moel y Don: Low Tide

Proposed landing beach at Moel y Don: Low Tide

On the day on the attack Tacitus records in:
Annales Book XIV, xxx

'On the shore stood the opposing army with its dense array of armed warriors, while between the ranks dashed women, in black attire like Furies, with hair dishevelled, waving brands.All around, the Druids, lifting up their hands to heaven and pouring forth dreadful imprecations, scared our soldiers by the unfamiliar sight, so that, as if their limbs were paralysed, they stood motionless and exposed to wounds. Then urged by their General's appeals and mutual encouragements not to quail before a troop of frenzied women, they bore the standards onwards, smote down all resistance, and wrapped the foe in the flames of his own brands. A force was next set over the conquered, and their groves, devoted to inhuman superstitions, were destroyed. They deemed it indeed a duty to cover their altars with the blood of captives and consult their deities through human entrails'

The planning would have had to have been meticulous for the attack to be successful, needing elite troops landing, and being able to hold and even expand the bridgehead to allow for more troops to be brought across. Therefore, to ensure that he could achieve this bridgehead he had to get a significant and effective force across the Strait as quickly as possible. In order to do this there were two key elements aside from tides and weather. Firstly he had to have sufficient boats to transport his troops across the tidal waterway and an effective strategy to endure that the first wave of troops landed with plenty of covering support to build and maintain a bridgehead to allow more troops to come across and force the 'enemy' back from the beach.

Overleaf is a photograph of Mona's shoreline today approximately 1.5 kms SW of Moel y Don (on the right in the background is Llanfair-is-gaer and beyond that the mountains of Snowdonia). Here it is a pebble and sand beach at low tide on which the Roman troops may well have landed on. The actual water channel is far over to the right along the mainland side of the Strait adjacent to Llanfair-is-gaer.

There are no records of how they got across the Strait but it is possible that the X1111 Legion did bring with it knowledge and expertise from their actions against the Germanic tribes when having to cross the river Rhine from their base at Mogontiacum (Mainz), the Romans favoured bridges but first they had to cross these large rivers in order to secure the opposite bank before contruction of a bridge coukld commence.

Tacitus does give us some idea of what occurred at this point in his:

Annales Book XIV, xxix

'...*he* [Governor Gaius Seutonius Paulinus] *therefore prepared to attack the island of Mona which had a powerful population and was a refuge for fugitives. He built flat-bottomed vessels to cope with the shallows, and uncertain of the depths of the sea. Thus the infantry crossed, while the cavalry followed by fording or, where the water was deep, swam by the side of their horses.*

This could be either the building a considerable number of small boats or much larger flat bottomed boats holding at least a centuria – a century (10 contubernium - 80 men plus a centurion) for the initial landings followed by supplies and replacements until the tide forced them to halt further sailings until the next appropriate tide. Though we do not have much idea as to the size of these flat bottomed boats there are a number of Roman built examples found in archaeological digs around Europe which are contemporary to this period and which may have been similar to those constructed and used at the Strait. The key was flat bottomed boats; they could be beached easily, refloated on the next tide (especially if the proposed landing site on Mona is correct) and stable enough to have had scorpio mounted on its deck as added protection.

Transport For the Beach Landings

There are no records of what boats were used but these Roman examples are contemporary to this time period in Europe.

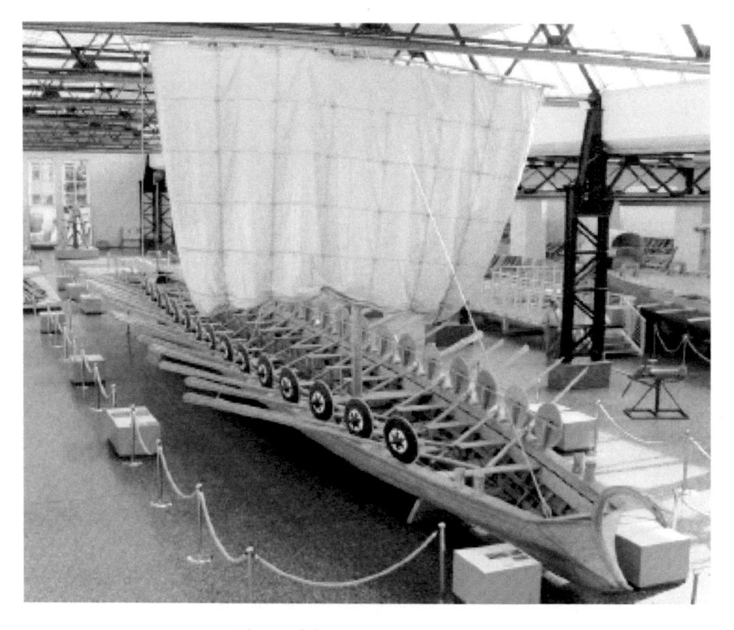

Roman Fluvial boat (Wikimedia Commons)

Above is a copy of a Roman Fluvial boat: a rapid intervention launch with a long narrow and shallow keel. Rowed by troops (16 oars per side). 5 such boats found in the mud of the Rhine at Mainz (Mogontiacum) in early 1980's.

The only other reference we have of Paulinus on Mona is in

History of Rome, Book LX11, pp 95-97, Cassius Dio
7. '......Boudicca led her army against the Romans; for these chanced to be without a leader, in as much as Paulinus, their commander, had gone on an expedition to Mona, an island near Britain...'
8. 'Now it chanced that Paulinus had already brought Mona to terms, and so on learning of the disaster of Britain, he at once set sail thither from Mona. ,,,'

Interestingly there is a clear reference to this episode in

The History of England, Vol., 1, pp 51-52, John Milton, 1670
'Seutonius Paulinus, who next was sent (after the death of Verannius) hither, esteemed a soldier, equal to the best in that age, for 2 years together went on prosperously, both confirming what he got, and subduing onward. At last, overconfident of his present actions, and emulating others, of whose deeds he heard from abroad, he marches up as far as Mona, the Isle of Anglesey, a populous place. For they, it seems, has both entertained fugitives and given good assistance to the rest that withstood him. He makes his boats with flat bottoms, filled in the shallows, which he expected in that narrow firth, his foot so passed over, his horse waded or swam. Thick upon the shore stood several gross bands of men, well weaponed, many women, like furies, running to and fro in dismal habit, with their hair loose about their shoulders, held torches in their hands. The Druids (those were their priests, of whom more in another place) with hands lifted up to heaven, uttering direful prayers, astonished the Romans, who, at such a strange sight stood in amaze, though wounded; but at length, awakened and encouraged by their general not to fear a barbarous and lunatic rout, fall on and beat

them down, scorched and rolling in their own fire. Then they yoked them with garrisons, and the places consecrated to their bloody superstitions destroyed. For whom they took to war, they held it lawful to sacrifice; and by the entrails of men used divination. While Paulinus had his thought still fixed before to go on winning, his back lay broad open to the occasion of losing more behind, for the Britons, urged and oppressed with many insufferable injuries, had all banded themselves to a general revolt'.

which appears to embellish Tacitus' account. Clearly the works of Tacitus were not confined to the dusty libraries of Rome.

In the description by Tacitus' in xxx on the previous page concerning the Roman troops '*....scared our soldiers by the unfamiliar sight, so that, as if their limbs were paralysed, they stood motionless and exposed to wounds*' (though the Druids and the Furies were some distance away on the opposing shore) it does beg the question as to why he should record this. Is it that Roman troops were reticent about crossing the Strait in the first place and having 'hoards of hostiles' clearly visible on the opposite bank did indeed put some fear into them. They had faced Celtic tribesmen before in battles as well as hit and run skirmishes, so the Romans knew how to fight them or was it the fear of the Druids and their Gods as they crossed into the 'home' of the Druids. These men were tried and tested men in battle on the land, they were not sailors and they saw what could potentially happen as they crossed over with the tribesmen throwing missiles at them from the shoreline. The fear is more likely to have been of drowning while crossing the Strait sea water. The fact that Paulinus sought to cajole and encourage his men across and with the cavalry by their side as they crossed they could overcome their fears and did break the 'paralysis' of fear and got them to go and defeat these 'frenzied women'. It also confirms that Paulinus decided that a day attack was the battle plan; daylight would have been the only way they could discern who was who over that sort of distance.

Proposed Map of Paulinus Invasion Across the Strait at Llanfair-is-gaer

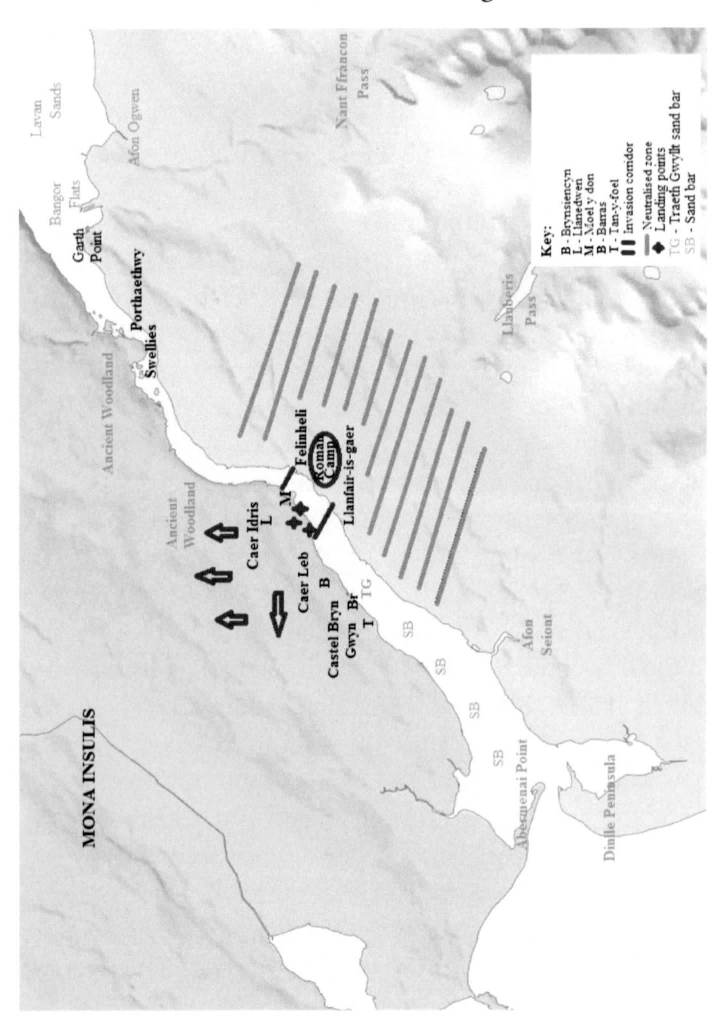

Caer Leb: area of 200' x 160' enclosed by 2 stoney banks and ditches.
Castell Bryn Gwyn: 180' in diameter enclosed by 12' high bank
Caer Idris: 36m x 80m elongated with 3 stoney banks, very poor condition
Caer Machod (close to Caer Leb at Llanidan): almost entirely destoyed but 1841 OS map shows 2 coniguous enclosures and round houses (archeological evidence found dating to Roman period)
None of the above have been identified as have being inhabited at the time of Paulinus and Agricola.

Having travelled a good deal of this stretch of the Strait it is difficult to believe Tacitus' description regarding the solders seeing '*a dense array of armed warriors with frenzied women dancing amongst them*' on the opposirte shoreline as correct. Today the distance is too great to clearly identify somebody on the opposite shore. It begs the question as to whether the Strait were either a lot narrower then or as is more plausible, he wrote it to deflect from the fear of troops in full armour crossing a moving expanse of water, not something that would enhance the reputation of Rome's armies.

Paulinus' encampment (see Proposed Map of Paulinus' Invasion overleaf) on the mainland would have had to have been secure from any attacks from the region to its rear so he is likely to have maintained a 'neutralised threat zone' so that they could concentrate all their efforts on the island. There is archaelogical evidence to show that there was human occupation in this region with a number of settlements but whether the area was heavily forested or the ground was being farmed is not known but it is likely that the Romans would have cleared a significant area as a defensive 'clear zone' and cutting trees for the construction

Caer Leb

Castell Bryn Gwyn

for boat building as well as ballista and scorpios.

In support of his vanguard troops on the first wave of boats he would have used artillery set near the shoreline:

- Onagers - with large stones (and could be covered with a comb-ustible material and set alight) could reach distances of between 275 m and 500 m
- Scorpios; precision shooting on a flat trajectory at 100 m and with parabolic shooting (the Scorpio angled upwards so that the bolts trajectory travelled in an arc towards its target) could reach 400 m, firing 3-4 bolts per minute. The weight and speed of these bolts would be sufficient to pierce the 'enemies' shield with devastating effect.

His troops would need this ballista cover as a screen while they were vulnerable during the crossing. If they were the larger type of transport boats he may well have have scorpios placed on board for extra protection to keep the tribesmen away from the shore as the boats grounded. We know nothing of the defences (if any) that the islanders may have constructed and what weapons they could use to assail the boats coming towards the shores. Hand held slingshots could have caused real problems for those on the boats and the cavalry swimming along with them as they came close to shore; there would hace certainly been a good supply of these small missiles on the beach line.probonst It is likely that the cavalry who were recorded as fording the Strait would have stayed relatively close to the boats for safety but also as protection for the troops while they were disembarking on to the shore of the island.

Once on land again it would be then up to the Roman soldiers discipline to rapidly get into battle formations that they had been rigourously trained in to keep them on the move against their 'enemy'. What they would not have known is what was behind the shoreline: large settlements or small farms close together or spread out over the island and where the Druid centres were. For a successful campaign they would have had to move swiftly and the destruction as they moved forward would have been thorough.

As Vegetius noted in the training of Roman army recruits '*No part of drill is more essential in action than for soldiers to keep their ranks with the greatest exactness, without opening or closing too much. Troops too much crowded can never fight as they ought, and only embarrass one another. If their order is too open and loose, they give the enemy an opportunity of penetrating. Whenever this happens and they are attacked in the rear, universal disorder and confusion are inevitable. Recruits should therefore be constantly in the field, drawn up by the roll and formed at first into a single rank. They should learn to dress in a straight line and to keep an equal and just distance between man and man. They must then be ordered to double the rank, which they must perform very quickly, and instantly cover their file leaders. In the next place, they are to double again and form four deep. And then the triangle or, as it is commonly called, the wedge, a disposition found very serviceable in action. They must be taught to form the circle or orb; for well-disciplined troops, after being broken by the enemy, have thrown themselves into this position and have thereby prevented the total rout of the army*'.

As the first troops were landing or certainly nearing the shore, the use of their scutum would have been paramount to their protection against thrown spears and slingshot. What they could not protect against would have been poor artillery shots from their own bank and there would have been losses as the artillery would have been aimed 'over the heads' of the troops in the boats. Once on land they would have rapidly formed a cohesive force probably forming up into testudos until sufficient numbers had landed and then formed into a wedge formation

The Testudo:

The front rank of the formation would kneel behind their interlocked scutum. The second rank would hold their scutum above the heads of the man in front of him and so on with the ranks behind them. If all round protection was needed, the men on the flanks and the rear could also present and lock their scutum together. These curved shields formed an excellent missile barrier as spears and slingshots rained down on them. This formation also allowed the troops beneath to advance as a unit or as a protection if outnumbered, whilst more troops disembarked.

Re-enactment of the testudo formation (Wikimedia Commons)

Re-enactment of the Wedge formation (Wikimedia Commons)

The Wedge

On the cry of *'cuneum formate'* the troops would have aligned themselves into a v- shaped wedge formations. The point of this wedge being a single soldier with his shield defending most of his body and his gladius free to cut and thrust in the gap between his sheild and the man's to his right just behind him (as would the man to his left) and so on (see page 84). This wedge would then drive forwards towards the enemy's shield wall as a concentrated killing machine and drive through their lines. Extra troops would be inside the formation to fill any gaps where men fell from the face of the wedge ensuring that the formation did not fail. The light cavalry would be on their flanks charging through and behind the enemy, rapidly breaking down any serious formation that the enemy could muster.It would have been a sight to behold; Roman soldiers lining up in organised formations, quiet and determined whilst the 'enemy' postured and shouted curses and taunting these invaders. To many of the islanders this would have been their first sight of Roman centurions.

In battle the tribes people were known to have used noise as a form of fear tactic against their opponents (something that many other civilisations had used in battle before and after this event) which does agree with Tacitus' statement of

'All around, the Druids, lifting up their hands to heaven and pouring forth dreadful imprecations....' it may well have also included curses from the warriors as well.

For those standing there on the shore of Mona facing this large force coming towards them this was much more than just fighting the Romans, they were fighting to save their way of life, their families, the home of their religion and their last refuge... an extremely powerful motive to fight much more fiercely and for many, to the death. However, because they were a confederation of 'family' groups and refugees, commanding them as a fighting force would have been near impossible.. a cohesive force working together against Roman troops was not going to happen, they were 'up against it' even before a blade was drawn and a spear thrown. Yet we have no idea of the number that faced these Romans.

As for the Romans, this was yet just another battle against people who would not accept their fate and be ruled by Rome. The 'voice' of war would not be heard from these well trained and disciplined Roman troops until they had actually engaged with the enemy, and keeping the battle formation would remain paramount until the enemy had been broken on the field of battle.

When ready and in range of the opposing enemy troops (10 to 15 meters) the Roman front ranks would have thrown their pila followed by the second ranks. It is then that with the noise of the cornu trumpets (blown by the cornicen) would have sounded out from the ranks of Roman troops giving the coded battlefield instructions from the general to his men that would have changed the scene from static formation to advancing on the 'enemy' still in formation leading to hand to hand fighting from behind their scutum. This sudden change in demeanour of the Romans and the volley of pila would have likely shocked and affected their enemy's morale already stunned by the deaths of many from the bombardment of bolts from the ballista and scorpio's.

Now the reality of the islanders (Druids, chieftains, warriors, farmers, women and slaves pressed into the fight) fate became starkly evident.They saw before them a wall of shields with short Roman swords thrust between, cutting and slashing the unprotected flesh of these defenders whilst they could not get to strike at these Romans would have been demoralising. These island defenders would have been constantly charging this advancing wall of sheilds attempting to break it down. It was here that the power of the Roman formation came into its own. Whether in a testudo or wedge formation each Roman soldier would have up to eight men behind him so that if the front man fell the shield wall would be filled instantly by the man behind him. Not only that each front row soldier could fight hard for up to 6 or eight minutes and then be replaced by the man behind him this gave each soldier time to recover (as much as 30 minutes if his comrades were not falling in front of him) from the intense effort before getting back into the fray. Unlike him island opponents who would get exhausted by being kept fighting on the sheild wall by the pressure of his tribe behind him trying to move forwards. They would eventually fall the to the blade of the gladius and falling under the feet of the advancing Romans and be 'finished' off if not already dead. Very soon the ground would be covered in blood, gore and other bodily fluids as the advance and killing continued. Seeing friends and family cut down as bodies, limbs and heads were hacked open would have struck fear into their very souls..

The intense trauma and stress of this close contact hand-to-hand fighting realistically meant that the combatants on both sides would not be fighting continuously; there would have been short periods of intense fighting followed by a short 'breathing' space lull if the fighting was proving indecisive. For the defenders it meant death, for the Roman troops who had perfected formations that would allow the individuals to do this. meant that there was little or no break in the fighting and they could maintain the pressure for many hours, steeling themselves for what they knew was to come but also knowing that they would win the day.

The island warriors and defenders would not have fought as a cohesive force, it was not there way and had probably not revised their form of warfare to deal with this Roman form of,war which was fighting continuously until they had won the battle. It was inevitable therefore that the Brythonic Celt line would not have been able to sustain intense fighting for very long and the carnage wrought by the Romans would break them sooner rather than later. When it did then those that had survived the initial battle would pay dearly. It is clear that Seutonious was intent on total destruction and no mercy would be shown, the killing would continue when the battle was over.

It is clear from Tacitus that in his description of this attack that no quarter was given and that total destruction was the order of the day...

'they smote down all resistance, and wrapped the foe in the flames of his own brands. A force was next set over the conquered, and their groves, devoted to inhuman superstitions, were destroyed. They deemed it indeed a duty to cover their altars with the blood of captives and consult their deities through human entrails'.

Given what Tacitus had written regarding actions of the Roman soldiers on this day, it can be taken that the 'enemy' broke and what followed was utter carnage ...men, women and probably children were all slaughtered. Those who looked for sanctuary in their sacred *Llwyn* (*Llanerch or Nemeton*) were killed and the Romans made sure that these groves would be their funeral pyres and so destroying the Druids, rebels and groves (*Llwyn*) in one fell swoop. There is archaeological evidence in the parish of Llanidan on the site at Bryn yr Hen Bobl of significant quantities of charcoal suggesting large fires (though there is no carbon dating information to date it). It has been identified as that of hazel, ash, oak and willow, all trees associated with the Druids!

The research came across some very colourful possible accounts (and probably not so far from the truth) of the horrors following the crossing as the Romans tracked down those enemy who had broken and fled the battlefield. One such is John Griffith's narrative in his article *'The Roman Invasion Of Anglesey – Silent Witness'* 2002. There is also *'Legion of the Eagles - Britannia'* 2015 by Simon Scarrow, a fictional story but based on classical accounts of actual Roman Legion battle tactics and which touches on the Roman invasion of Mona. Both seem in tune with written accounts of other Roman battles across the Roman Empire, where no quarter had been given e.g. the annihilation of the *Sugambri* tribe in Gaul.

The ferocity with which the Roman troops seem to have acted may be from orders given by their officers to finally and ruthlessly crush any resistance to Roman control in Britannia. It may also be from a sense of revenge and anger; remembering the fear they showed on the shoreline before the crossing, once they knew that they won the battle. The people of Mona were no match for these hardened Roman troops. Many place names are linked to historical events throughout history and that is no different in Mona. On early OS maps (19th C) of Anglesey and even today there are place names around the area where this invasion could have taken place which could quite easily bare a reference to these events. In the parish of Llanidan, just to the NW of the 'landing site' (see page 170) there are 2 fields known as *'The Field of the Long Battle'*[1]and *'The Field of Bitter Lamentation'*[1]. There is Bryn-y-Beddau, (*bryn*: hill; *beddau*: graves) just to the south of Porthamel. There are place names such as Plas Coch (*Coch*: red), Cae Coch all within 1¼ miles (2 km) of the proposed 'landing point'... a coincidence, a quirk of the millennia of history after the event or maybe a lasting memory of the slaughter that took place here.

Interestingly, it is only at the point in his writings that we see any clear mention of the Druids activities regarding human sacrifice on their altars. Was this a justification, after the event, for the level of violence that the Roman troops levelled on these inhabitants? Truly a case of the victor writing the story! After this initial rout the troops will have moved off the battle site and fanned out across the island. The primary targets would have been against the more populated areas along the island side of the strait to ensure that they were not outflanked by any reserve resistance fighters before moving across the island destroying and killing all before them. How long the troops spent on the killing spree, the destruction of the groves or how far they fanned their attack across the island is not known. As the date or month of the attack was not recorded there is no way to determine the length of his presence on the island.

As part of his military tactics it would have been prudent of Paulinus to move his command post or at the

---

[1] *'The Roman Invasion Of Anglesey' by John Griffiths 2002*

very least a staging post onto the island itself from where fresh troops could be deployed in follow up operations and exhausted troops could rest, eat and receive any medical attention. Was there any trace of such a place in this area? Erosion over the millenia and farming practices may well have obliterated any signs of a temporary camp but the finding of a site near Llanedwen close to the proposed invasion site in 2012 by the Gwynedd Archaeological Trust may have some bearing on this. Archaeological evidence found at the site revealed an unusual amount of high status material suggesting a Roman site linked to the Roman military. Coins and pottery analysis suggest 1st to 4th Century, road works and buildings but no sign of any defensive ditches. Does this have links to the Paulinus landings? Could it have been the site of a temporary command camp after the successful landings?

Many survivors of the battle and indeed any inhabitants of the area would have fled to safety into the woods and lands to the north and west of the island with Roman troops hunting them down. What we do know is that in mid-summer Paulinus received news that violence on a huge scale had broken out in the south east: Boudicca and the tribes of the Iceni, Trinovantes and others had risen up against their Roman oppressors and gone on a rampage of death and destruction against all that was Roman. Paulinus was so absorbed in his attack on Mona that he seems to have overestimated the extent to which the province he governed had been 'pacified', together with the moving of the XX Legion from Camulodunum to Glevum he had dangerously weakened the Roman forces in the south east. He also seemed content to have left his administration in the hands of his Procurator, Catus Decianus, and any incidents that required force could be dealt with by the military veterans (Colones).

From the classical text Paulinus appears to have reacted quickly and rushed back leaving Mona without completing his campaign. In Dio's text, he states that on hearing the news of the rebellion Paulinus *'at once set sail thither from Mona'*, a little poetic licence by Dio possibly but Paulininus' best course of action and probably fastest for him and his troops was to return the way they came and onto the lowlands towards Viroconium where he would have sent out a call to arms to all the Roman veterans in the region to join him and crush the rebellion unfolding in the south. An interesting question here is how quickly from when he was told of the uprising was he able to bring his 'rampaging' troops back into formation and back over the Strait for the rapid return journey to deal with the Boudicca and her huge army.

It would have been evident to him if he did not act immediately he could lose the whole of this Roman province, a situation he would take as an insult not only on his governorship but personally. He would show no mercy and it would be more severe than he had inflicted on the people of Mona!

The island had been reprieved, it would not face total destruction. The survivors of the rout and the remainder of the population of the island would have begun to care for their wounded and bury the dead, but their hatred of the Romans would endure. The loss of so many of their Druids, sacred groves and brave men and women would have been something that would live long in their memories.

Little of that destruction would be left over the millennia but there are tantalising hints in place names that still exist in that area today :

Whether they (and the other named fields in the Llanidan Parish) actually bare witness to the events of that time can only be a matter of conjecture, but given the Roman soldiers reputation for death and destruction in battle in the Celtic wars on mainland Europe, it should not be dismissed out of hand.

The story of the defeat of Boudicca and the rebels by Seutonius Paulinus and his soldiers is well known and they were was indeed merciless on the battlefield and in its aftermath. As for the Procurator, Catus, whose actions were very likely the trigger for the rebellion, he had fled to Gaul when the rebellion erupted.

The new Procurator, Gaius Julius Alpinus Classicianus, expressed concerns to Emperor Nero that the punitive measures that Paulinus was inflicting on the tribes of south east Britannia would lead to continued hostilities. There was no mention of the destruction on Mona!

In response Nero, who must have taken this seriously, sent his freedman, Polyclitus, to lead an enquiry. Paulinus was relieved of his command under the guise of him losing some ships, but he had kept Britannia in the hands of the Romans so they were not going to punish him too severely. He returned to Rome, but not in disgrace, he is depicted on victory columns in Rome with Nero, a clear indication that his actions in Britannia had clearly been honoured by the Emperor.

Paulinus does surface again in the classical texts, appearing on the general staff of Emperor Marcus Salvius Otho (AD 69 the year of the 4 Emperors) at the Battle of Bedriacum in northern Italy. They were engaged against Legate Aulus Vitellius who also had claim the throne of Rome, Paulinus in this case had advised Otho not to fight until they had more troops but Otho carried on (Paulinus is reported to have held he troops back at the battle) and they lost. Paulinus was captured but gained a pardon claiming he had deliberately lost the battle for Otho.

Authors Notes:

The destruction of the Druid groves and the death of so many Druids does not appear to have resulted in any great misfortune or execution for Seutonius Paulinus.

As for the XIIII Legion (now with the extended cognomen of Gemina Martia Victrix, the Victrix added after their successful defeat of the Boudican forces), it left the shores of Britannia in AD 67, briefly returning in 69 only to leave again in AD 70 and never return. For the Legion too nothing calamitous was recorded as having occured to it in the years that followed.

In the matter of Roman's crossing point on the Strait it would not be the last time that this proposed area would see an attack across the water. In 1282 during Edward 1's campaign against the Welsh, English forces under the command of Luke de Tany bridged the Strait with boats at low tide between Felinheli/Porth Dinorwig and Moel y Don in order to get his troops across quickly in an attempt to crush the Welsh 'rebels' on Mona. Unfortunately for the English they were beaten back by the Welsh soldiers and forced back to the bridge which was by that time under great stress from the rising tide. Many of the fleeing soldiers were lost crossing the bridge as it broke apart before they reached the other side.

The Aftermath and Intervening Years: AD 69 to AD 78

The ferocity of death and destruction on the lives and property which Paulinus' reprisals smeated out on the tribes of south east Britannia during and after the Boudican revolt would have shaken all the peoples of Britannia, including Mona, to the core. If the Romans were not careful they could still lose Britannia: continued action by Paulinus could have led other tribes (including the 'Rome friendly' *Brigantes*) to rise up in arms against such an oppressive Governor.

Fortunately, Rome and Emperor Nero had listened to the plea from Procurator Classicianus and the report from the freedman Polyclitus. Nero decided that his 'heroic' Governor Paulinus should be brought back to Rome and a new Governor appointed. The new man would rebuild its destroyed towns, restore trading links and improve tribal relations. Rome needed the grain and the metals that Britannia had ... no more heavy handed treatment of the 'locals', but just to be on the safe side and knowing that the revolt had shown the Roman troops weakness in armed troop numbers, he sent 9 more auxiliary legions with the new Governor as insurance against any further 'problems'. Petronius Turpilianus took over from Paulinus in AD 62/3, and as Tacitus records *'he neither challenged the enemy or was molested himself'*.

There are varying estimates as to how many Britons were killed in the action against Boudicca's forces because of the number of tribes involved but of those on Mona there are none. It can only be surmised that the halting of the destruction and killings on the island was not complete because of the Romans were called back urgently to deal with Boudicca (needing all their forces to defeat the threat in the south) and there is no mention of a return on the orders of Paulinus to 'finish the job'. It is likely there were some survivors left on the island who would fled towards Holy Island but it is also probable that most if not all the Druidic places would have been destroyed. Those that were left would have had to dig graves (possibly mass graves if whole families had been killed) for those bodies that were not burned in their houses or the Druid groves.

Though many of the most vociferous and active opponents of Roman rule on the island may well have been killed a few will have suvived along with some Druids. Now would have been the time to 'lick the wounds' and keep a low profile. They needed peace in order to rebuild their lives just to survive. The loss of so many may well have meant either no crops sown or there were not enough people left to harvest the crops for the coming winter. Any thought of continuing any resistance would have been left for a later day.

Governor Tuilianus was succeeded in AD 63 by Marcus Trebellius Maximus who carried on the 'softly softly' approach. This govenor had no military experience, Tacitus noting that *'he kept the province in hand by a mild mannered administration'*. However auxiliary legions were sent to Britannia to replace the relocation of the XIIII Legion to Germania in AD 67.

There are no record of Roman troops being stationed on Mona during this period, and there is no current archaeological definitive evidence to suggest that they were there.

Following the death of Emperor Nero in AD 68 (assisted suicide) and Rome and rule over the empire was thrown into turmoil. Galba was emperor from June AD 68 until Jan AD 69 when he was assainated (on orders from

Otho!). He was quickly followed by Otho who reigned for 3 months before he committed suicide after being defeated in battle against Aulus Vitellius. Then Vilellius became emperor and reigned from April AD 69 until Dec AD 69 (he was assassinated) – it would be known as the year of the 4 Emperors.

It was Vitellius who had appointed Vettius Bolanus as the governor of Britannia in AD 69 (following Trebillius's departure to Europe), and he sent the Legio XIIII with him (they had been aligned to Otho so the Emperor wanted them out of the way). Bolanus was also fully aware that the upheavals and political manoeuvrings and legion allegiances could trigger another rebellion in Brittania. Which is why he refused to send troops to Rome when Emperor Vitellius' requested them. With the Roman hierarchy in turmoil it was a good opportunity to rise up against Rome rule but it appears that 'resistance' in Britannia as a whole had indeed been crushed for the foreseeable future. In fact Governor Bolanus seems only to have faced one major issue and that was the second insurrection of King Venutius of the Brigantes. Queen Cartimandua, ex-wife of Venutius, had been a loyal client ruler for twenty years. The Romans had defended her against an earlier revolt by her ex-husband. On this occasion, however, Bolanus was only able to send auxiliaries to her aid. Cartimandua was evacuated, leaving the kingdom to Venutius. Siding with Rome and giving them Caratacus had eventually lost her the kingdom.

Nothing more is recorded concerning Mona or the activities of the Druid's. For those Druids who had survived, would they have started the seats of learning again? Would they have sent out desperate pleas to 'past' students who had completed their 20 year training and gone to other parts of Britannia (or even further afield into Celtic

Europe) to return and rebuild the Druid 'university'?

It may well have been that many of the Druid 'lore masters' and teachers had been killed during this attack, leaving a huge and very likely incalculable effect on the very core of Druidic culture and its teachings...

There are no records in the classical texts of any attacks on Druids anywhere else in Europe or Britannia during this period so it was not an all out attack on their religious rites and practices. Tacitus writings appear to have been the main the main source of information on this period before the invasion of Britannia and it may be that there were events concerning the Druids of mainland Europe that were recorded in the missing books. The assault by Paulinus on Mona was not completed, so those who had fled to the north and north west of the island were spared by the Roman troops being withdrawn. The fact that Roman troops were not recorded as having returned later to the island does suggest that the Roman governors believed that all resistance had been crushed in AD 69.

In order to to reduce any provocation and try and keep the 'peace' on the western border, Trebellius had the XX Legion moved back from the Usk to Glevum and then on to Viroconium. However the Legion who had spent years fighting and being badly mauled by the *Silures* saw this as a retreat, not a peace keeping move. Their anger flared up and they revolted against him as Governor. Having lost the loyalty of the Legion he fled to Europe in fear of his life.

In AD 71 a new governor was appointed to Britannia, Quintas Petilus Cerealis (who had been Legate of the Legio IX Hispana at the time of the Boudican revolt), and on his staff was Julius Agricaola who would become Legate of the Legio XX. He had already served under Paulinus in action against Mona in AD 69.

Cerealis now had to deal with the Brigantes under King

Venutis who were openly opposing Roman rule. He had the Legio II Adiutrix follow him from Rome. It was founded by Emperor Vespasian in AD 70 and originally made up of Roman navy marines, mainly from Egypt, from the eastern Mediterranean fleet at Ravenna (where they had faced no naval threat). During the next few years this legio would stay in Britannia and subdue the rebel tribes in western and northern Britannia, with a base camp in or near Deva – inscriptions on tablets of soldiers from this Legio found in the area confirm this, see below:

-***Gaius Calventius*** Gai filius Claudia tribu Celer Apro miles **legionis II Adiutricis** Piae Fidelis / Vibi Clementis (...). Chester, U.K. RIB 475.
- ***Gaius Iuventius*** Gai filius Claudia tribu Capito Apro / miles **legionis II Adiutricis** Piae Fidelis / Iuli Clementis annorum XL stipendiorum XVII. Chester, U.K. RIB 476
- ***Lucius Terentius*** Claudia tribu Fuscus Apro miles **legionis II Adiutricis** Piae Fidelis. Chester, U.K. RIB 477.
- ***Gaio Valerio Crispo*** veterano ex **legione II Adiutrice** Pia Fideli. Chester, U.K. RIB 478.

The Roman encampment at Deva appears to have been establishhed as part of a series of new forts to ensure 'co-operation' in the assimilation of the already 'romanised' tribes into the Roman empire. Was this a perceived threat from the lands to the north, the Brigantes, or from the tribes to the west?

These years of civil war 'distraction' in Rome and amongst the Brigantes had given both the *Silures* and the *Ordovices* a period of respite, and it is more than likely that they would have begun to re-establish their independence with no obvious interference from the Roman governor.

However in AD 74 Sextus Julius Frontius was

appointed Governor and things were about to change. He was a military man to the core and a very successful strategist who would use these skills to continue the 'subjugation' that Cerealis had started. The Brigantes problem had been dealt with (for now) and forts were now in place to 'control' any situations, but there was still the matter of western Brittania to deal with. It is not clear from the classical texts as to whether there was any specific incident that lead to the concerted effort to break and control these western Britannic tribes, it may be that raiding had begun again and skirmishes with Roman troops had been on the rise. There was the attracation of gold mines at Dolaucothi, and copper in the Great Orme at Llandudno and Parys Mountain on Mona (Ref.Fig on page 195)

What is in no doubt though, is that Governor Frontius carried out a successful campaign against the Silures and the tribes of eastern 'Wales' (*Ordovicians* and *Deceangli*?) which he completed by AD 77. The strategies he utilisied were later recorded in his book *'Stratgematicon Libri Quattour'*, written towards the end of his life (he died in AD 103): a book primarily of military stategies used in battles in both Greek and Roman history.

He, as Cerealis had done in the Briganates territory, now carried out a program of establishing new forts at strategic points in this region: river crossings and crossroads, enabling easier control of movement in the areas. A new legion fortress was established at Isca Silurum for the Legio II Augusta, along with forts at Deva (Chester), Segontium, Levobrinta, Mediomanum, Circucium, Castell Collen (Powys), Coelbren (west Glamorgan) and camps at Blaen-cwm-bach (west Glamorgan), Twyn-y-Briddallt (mid Glamorgan) and Pen-y-Coed (mid Glamorgan). It appears to be the beginnings of a network of forts 15-20 kms apart maintained by auxiliary units to maintain the peace and order. See page 195.

Parys Mountain

Cemlyn Bay

It is interesting to read that Tacitus wrote of Julius Frontius *'he was equal to the burden, a great man as far as greatness was then possible, who subdued by his arms the powerful and warlike tribe of the Silures, surmounting the difficulties of the country as well as the valour of the enemy'*. He clearly recognised the *Silures* as a powerful foe!!

Who was directly responsible for each fort construction is more difficult to determine as dateable evidence was not prolific and many of the finds were outside the confines of the walls. It is also quite possible that there were other forts at strategic points but these has been lost to history with changes in farming techniques, erosion and even rivers changing course.

There are Roman forts and attributable structures on Mona; Caer Tŵr (Watch Tower) on Holyhead Mountain overlooking the harbour, and possibly the remains of a small Roman fort in Holyhead (part of which is still visible in the walls of St Cybi's churchyard).

In 2015 a small Roman style fort was discovered on land near Cemlyn Bay close to the Wylfa Power Station by the Gywnedd Archaeological Trust. Described as a fortlet surrounded by a circular ditch and reportedly dating back to the 1st Century AD (earlier than those of the remains in Holyhead which date to the 3rd Century). What is curious is that considering Mona has supposedly been a 'nest' of resistance there appears to have been no concerted plan in the construction of forts on the island to 'control' the population. Had Agricola done a deal with the island chieftains so that they could retain a relative autonomy from direct Roman rule. As for the mainland it is clear that the 'lattice' work of forts they had constructed controlled much of the land. The military points connected by new Roman roads allowed the rapid deployment of troops wherever they may have been required. They also provided

Iron age Huts on Holyhead Mountain

Holyhead Mountain

a better transport system to and from valuable metal mines (indicated on the map overleaf as G - gold and C – copper)

AD 78 saw Frontius retired to Rome and a soldier who had already experienced battles against the tribes of southern Britannia during its inasion, fought with Paulinus in the attack on Mona and in charge of the XX Legion under Cerialis would become the new Governor of Britannia.

The Roman Forts of Frontius and Agricola

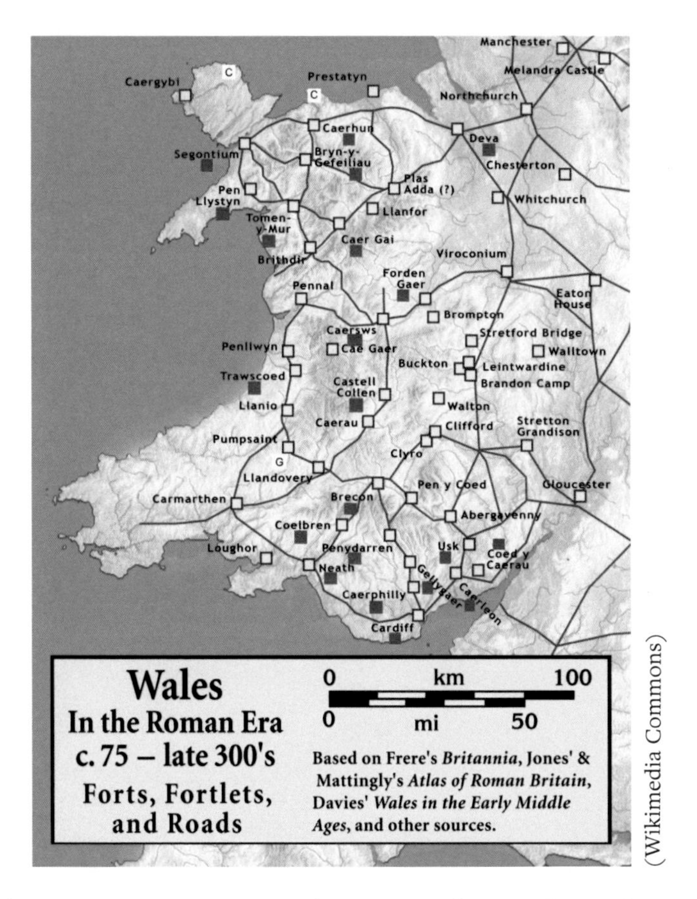

(Wikimedia Commons)

The RED SQUARES on the map indicate those forts established and attributed to **Sextus Julius Frontius** and **Gaius Julius Agricola** in western Britannia between AD 74 and AD 79. They were quite clearly put in place to readily control the lands of the *Silures* and *Ordovicians.* The *Demetea* in the south west seem to have not been an issue considering there are so few forts in their lands.

Governor Gaius Julius Agricola: AD 78- 84

Statue representing Agricola located at the Roman baths in Aquae Sulis
(Wikimedia Commons)

Much of what we know about Agricola is accounts by the Roman historian Tacitus, who just happened to be Agricola's son-in-law. So when reading the accounts of Agricola's actions in Britannia (as well as in Rome) there has to be some modicom of suspicion that he may be slightly inflating his father-in-laws position and achievements. Having said that he did serve in the Roman army in Brittania very effectively and did become a successful governor. In order to understand his future actions in Brittania it is necessary to know a little of the man before he became governor.

As has already been related, Agricola's first venture into Britannia was as a military tribune (a Roman officer who ranked below the legate and above the centurion - young men of Equestrian rank often served as military tribune as a stepping stone to a political career in the Roman Senate). He served with Seutonius Paulinius in the first attack on Mona.

As Tacitus recounts *'he served his military apprenticeship to the satisfaction of Seutonius Paulinus, a painstaking and judicious officer, who, to test his merits, selected him to share his tent. .. He sought to make himself acquainted with the province and known to the army; he would learn from the skilful, and would keep pace with the brave, would attempt nothing for display, would avoid nothing for fear and would be at once careful and vigilant'*. This was a man who was not using the role of tribune just a means to an end, he wanted to learn to be a good soldier and a leader of men.

Following the defeat of Boudicca he returned to Rome and followed the path of politics. There he met and happily married a highborn lady which gave this ambitious man advancement and distinction. He was appointed Quaestor (a low-ranking magistrate) for Asia with the corrupt Salvius Titianus as his Proconsul - a path that Julius did not engage in. He then was made a Praetor, still under Nero's Rome, and continued to do his work as he had when in the army.

The death of Nero led to choas of the year of the 4 Emperors. Agricola was appointed by Galba to account for temple offerings! AD 69 saw a serious blow to Agricola when Otho's fleet attacked Intenelii, a district of Liguria where his mother lived and she was murdered and his estate plundered. He set out to deal with the situation when word came of Vespasian's declaration for the Emperor's seat. Agricola joined his cause and for his loyalty he was appointed (and quite probably because of his knowledge of Britannia and its tribes strengths and weaknesses) as a Legate and sent to Brittania to command the XX Legion. The Legion had been slow to take the oath of allegiance to Vespasian and its commander, Roscius Coelius was reportedly acting disloyally (they had been moved from their positions on the river Usk to Glevum by Governor Bolanus – see earlier reference). A role which surely tested his abilities as a soldier and commander to winning over a disaffected Legion.

Under the new Governor Cerealis, according to Tacitus, he was an obedient and honourable soldier. The governor at first had him involved in his campaigns and eventually gave him command of part of the forces but Agricola remained subordinate to the successes of his commander, and in so doing enjoyed the victories without raising his profile too high where 'others jealousy would become apparent'. When Cerealis' had completed his term as Governor he returned to Rome and Julius Agricola soon followed. Agricola had proved himself to Emperor Vespasian who then promoted him to the Patrician order and gave him the province of Aquitania.

A role again he took to well; he proved to be a man of '*good sense*' as Tacitus remarks '*without harshness, pride, or the greed of gain, and his good nature did not weaken his authority nor strictness*' which he had already shown when taking command of the XX Legion.

With the retirement of Frontius it appears that Emperor Vespasian saw Agricola as the ideal replacement because of his loyalty to the Emperor and his previous good military service in Britannia.

So in AD 78 Gaius Julius Agricola was duly appointed Governor of Britannia.

The Second Attack on Mona: AD 78

Agricola landed on Britannia's shores in late summer of AD 78. From the classical texts it appears that the troops who had been led by Frontius felt that their work of subjugation was almost complete. They had begun to relax their vigilance, especially as it was coming close to the end of the campaigning season and return to barracks for the winter. The tribes people would also have believed that they would be left alone for a while.

However it appears that Frontius had not yet tackled the tribes in the north western area of Britannia, the *Ordovices* (or a confederacy of these northern tribes - *Deceangli, Ordovices, Gangani* and the inhabitants of Mona), and they were about to get a rude awakening. The incident that triggered the Roman action is shrouded in mystery; there is no recorded detail on the attack and the killing of a squadron[1] of Roman cavalry or where it actually occurred, but news reached Agricola at his headquarters that a the unit had been nearly wiped out when the tribesmen had attacked a fort they were quartered in and was inside Ordovician territory. Searching the records there does not appear to be a known Roman fort that would fit this scenario. There are no clearly identified auxiliary forts in the region but it is believed that most of the outpost forts were manned by auxiliary units (auxiliary troops were now nearly in equal numbers to Roman troops). Most of these

---

[1]*Tacitus describes it as a 'squadron' but in the Imperial Roman military this term was never used. A basic unit was a TURMAE – consisting of 32 troopers under the command of a Decurion. An ALAE (WING) – consisted of 512 men (16 Turmae),; it was this size of cavalry unit that would normally have manned auxiliary forts on the borders - acting as scouts, information gatherers and a 'reaction' force against any unrest in the area.*

forts are recorded as having been set up by Frontius in this region as most of his campaigns (according to Tacitus) were aimed against the Silures in the south and midlands. Apparently, this incident shows then this was not the case. Though Roman forts in the north have been attributed to Agricola's governorship in line with his military actions it seems that at least one fort was already in existence prior to his arrival in Britannia for it to be attacked.

Whatever the reason for this serious action by the tribesmen it is more than probable that other tribesmen watched to see what the reaction of the new governor would be... was another rebellion possible if this governor chose not to act??

In order to destroy a unit of cavalry (whether it be 32 or 500 men) it would more than likely have been an ambush (the usual tactic) and they would have needed a good number of men. They would then have retreated back to a place of safety and waited for any resulting backlash from the new Governor, which being late in the year would now probably be in the spring/summer of the following year. As was noted earlier, many of the Roman troops and the Auxiliaries had already returned to their winter quarters spread out all over the region, so pulling a large force together would prove difficult. He was probably advised by his officers that they should just man the weak points and face any further actions should it occur.

Agricola had not long been in Britannia but he needed to act and would have clearly considered his options:-

- it was getting late in the year and the weather would start to deteriorate
- making the gathering and moving of troops harder to achieve.
- supplies for a large force would take time to bring together and probably not be completed before winter set in.

- he had no fleet of ships he could call on a short notice for transport to the island.
- to delay until the new year was not an option. He had to act and impose his authority over the whole region or trouble may flare up again.

His most obvious route would have been travelling up from Londinium to Viroconium and then using the route known to him via the Llangollen pass. Using the same route suggested for the first invasion by Paulinus was not practical as the weather at that time of year in the mountains would have been poor.

He needed his troops as battle worthy as possible, so the route via Betws-y-coed and down the Conwy valley to the coast would have been the most practical but not without its problems. The coastal route would require negotiating around mountains into the sea (at Penmaenbach and Penmaenmawr) where no land ward route was practical.

Agricola would have been resolved to act... he had to stamp his authority on these tribes or risk the situation escalating. So he gathered together a *'force of veterans and a small body of auxiliaries'* and went after the rebels. These 'rebels' responsible for the attack were encamped on a hill (it is not clear whether it was a hill fort or not) and who refused to engage with the Roman troops. Not wanting to lose the impetus of this situation he led his troops up the hill, attacked the rebels and as Tacitus puts it *'all but exterminated the tribe'*.

There is a place that might fit this scenario: a possible refuge for these attackers and from where Agricola could have carried on to the Menai Strait. Braich y Dinas (*braich:* ridge; *dinas:* fort) – an extensive hill fort at the seaward end of the Conwy Valley at the summit of Penmaemawr (one of the northernmost peaks of the Carneddau mountain range on the North Wales coast). It measured approximately 4.4 ha (11 acres) containing some 100 houses with up to 3 m high outer walls. Excavations carried out by Harold Hughes in 1877 identified 1st and 2nd century AD Roman artefacts but also pre-Roman Iron age spindle-whorls and an Iron Age bronze brooch. The killing of a few rebels on a hill as Tacitus stated would not consitute *'all but exterminating the tribe'* but successfully attacking a fort that would have held a large group of men, women (young and old) and children and putting them all to the sword could be seen as destroying a large section of a tribe. Unfortunately the fort itself has been mainly lost due to quarrying later in the 19th Century after the 1877 site investigation had been carried out. This military action and his landing site on the island are suggestions based on circumstantial evidence at best ... there is no record as to where he started this venture from and his route to and onto Mona and where exactly any battles took place.

If we accept the word of Tactitus for what occurred, then having dealt with the tribe that carried out the killings, Agricola now looked to Mona. It is possible that he gained intelligence from a prisoner captured after the defeat of the tribe, that the attack had been instigated/planned on the island. Agricola would have known that Paulinus' attack in AD 68 had not been completed because of the Boudicca uprising. Being left in peace there would have been a resurgence of dissent amongst the islanders against the Romans. He would now have to follow up on his actions and put fear into all the remaining tribesmen and deal with those who responsible for killing his auxiliaries and to completely subjugate Mona.

Note: *In all texts regarding Agricola and his campaigns against the Ordovicians or the island of Mona there is no mention of the*

Druids or their practices. Roman action clearly seems to have been be against the tribesmen alone. This raises the pertinent question of where were the Druids?. Had they lost all influence within the tribal system or where there so few of them left after the AD 68 massacre that they were lost to history?

As Tacitus recounts, his decision was made '*he* [Agricola] *collected detachments of several Legions and a moderate force of native auxiliaries*' presumably a mobile force who could move quickly and '*after being disencumbered of all baggage, he picked a body of native men who knew the shallows and had national experience in swimming and by means of which they can controlsimultaneously their own movements, weapons and their horses. He then launched them upon the enemy so suddenly that the astonished islanders promptly came to the conclusion that nothing was hard and nothing invincible to men who fought in this fashion. Accordingly they petitioned for peace and surrendered the island*'. Meaning that he was now using Britannic tribesmen in his auxiliary forces or descendants of Batavian and Thracian troops who had joined the Roman army and still maintained the skills of their parents and grandparents. There may well have been local men who knew the waters also serving in the cavalry or acting as scouts (the Roman army paid well) or who were engaged locally by him (forcefully or not) when he arrived at the Strait.

We know that this 'rapid reaction force' that Agricola led did attack Mona, yet there is no record as to where he and his men crossed the Strait. From his time spent with Paulinus at the first invasion of the island he would have been privy to the intelligence gathered on the crossing points, the running of the tides and with his '*men that knew the shallows of these waters*' he may well have chosen the shorter, most advantageous and possibly dangerous route.

There was the need to carry out this action as quickly as possible before winter set in. To attempt a crossing again where Paulinus had crossed would take too long and alert the islanders to his presence. Horsemen and swimming troops had proved their worth in the first crossing so it could be done again and with not having to support infantry would make the landing and advancing into Mona much quicker.

The mention of '*the shallows*' in Tacitus' account could easily describe the area known as the Lafan sands[1] (a large area of intertidal sand and mudflats) and channel at the NE end of the Strait which at low tide was used to cross over to the island at a place now known as Beaumaris. [*See Aerial photograph on next page*].

At low tide (slack water at Beaumaris is around 4 and 5 hours before High Water) the deep water channel runs along the mainland side of the Strait up passed the 'Swellies' and moves across near Garth Point to the island side along passed what we now know as Beaumaris and on towards Penmon at the very NE end of the island. The narrowest point of this channel today is opposite Beaumaris. As has been discussed before the shifting sands of the Strait means that this has to be a matter of conjecture when considering 2000 years ago. As there does not appear, geologically, to have been any major changes to the area of the Strait and tidal levels have not changed significantly the

---

[1] *'Here at low water the Menai shrinks to a narrow channel, at which between Mona and the mainland extends a tract four miles broad, called the Lafan sands, reported to have been once cultivated ground. There is a ferry across the channel and the sands are passable on foot, with a guide, at low water. This is a frequented route from Beaumaris into Caernarfonshire though dangerous from the shifting nature of the sands and the chance of being overtaken by fog or tide' ...*

Penny Magazine of the Society for the Diffusion of Useful Knowledge, Vol 7-8, pp290, 1846

Low Tide at the north east end of the Strait. Right hand lower corner is the Bangor Flats, above that is the freshwater channel of Afon Ogwen and middle right is the expanse of the Lafan sands. Mona is on the left, Gallows Point is in the centre and the beach above it is adjacent to Beaumaris and beyond in the distance Penmon and the island of Ynys Seiriol.
Photograph courtesy of An Gariad Môn Wordpress.com.

deep water channels would probably not have changed significantly either.

Looking at the geography of this area it is more likely that if he did cross the sands here it would have been away from the outfalls of the Afon Cegin and Afon Ogwen from the mainland onto the Bangor Flats, the mixture of silt from these rivers and the the tidal sands. A horse and rider crossing around the Swellies, opposite Pothaewythy or from Garth Point may have been dangerous because of the currents and underwater hazards.

Today deep water channels from Porthaethwy up past Garth Point and on to Beaumaris exist with the depth at low

View from the mainland at low tide looking over to Beaumaris showing the extent of the Lafan sands

water ranging around 10 feet (UK Maritime Charts), though there is a much deeper area around Beaumaris. At low tide the water channel narrows in the area and could have been crossed by a trained force.

Agricola may well have had men and horses of his specialised Auxillaries swim across the channel between the Lafan sands and Gallows Point in a surprise attack and then capturing the ferry crosssing at Porthaethwy. He and his main force then would cross by ferry boats enabling them to carry out an unchallenged crossing to the island. Agricola, unlike Paulinus, had the advantage of surprise on his side going to Mona at this time of year when normally Roman military action would have stopped until the following Spring. With this 'strike' force it is unlikely he would have committed it all to the sands crossing and instead used a 'commando' style incursion to gain the upper hand quickly and decisively followed by the main force.

Was the island attacked a second time by a cleverly devised 'commando' style attack by the Romans that caught the rebel leaders out so thoroughly that they believed any further rebellion would be crushed before it had begun? In this 'invasion' of Mona there are no texts recording any fighting between Agricola's forces and the inhabitants on the island so it would seem that punishment and death for those that resisted Roman authority was not the order of the day it had been a bloodless invasion!upper hand quickly and decisively followed by the main force.

Tacitus records that '... *the astonished enemy were looking for a fleet, a naval armament and assault by sea, thought that to such assailants nothing could be formidable or invincible*'. Once on Mona it is not known where he confronted the 'leaders' or cheiftains of the island inhabitants (there is archaeological evidence of hill forts at Parciau and Bwrdd Arthur and settlements at the NE end of the island) but they must have sued for peace as there is no mention of any fighting, MONA INSULIS was now fully in the hands of Rome. He had done the unexpected and stunned the islanders into submission.

There are some issues with Tacitus' account of the Britannia's history concerning this particular attacks on Mona which are puzzling. He may have had limited information on Paulinus and his invasion due to the fact that many of the Roman combatants had more than likely passed away (as his book had been written over 30 years after the event), however as far as the 2nd is concerned, Cornelius Tacitus (born circa AD 56) married Julia Agricola (Gaius Julius Agricola's daughter) circa AD 77/78, possibly just before her father left to serve as the Governor of Britannia (which could explain his arrival in the province late in the year). Agricola completed his term in Britannia in AD 84 and returned to Rome. Tacitus is believed to have

Din Llugwy

Cromlech Llugwy

Din Silwy / Bwrdd Arthur

Aberffraw

Felinheli from Moel y Don

Beaumaris Castle and estuary

Llanidan

Dinas Gynfor

published his first book *'De vita lulii Agricola'* – trans. as 'The Life of Agricola' in AD 98 (the book that would have taken him a few years to write in order to ensure that no offence was caused to the living) – Agricola died in AD 93.

As Tacitus never ventured anywhere near Britannia it is fair to say that he must have gained much of the information recorded in his books from his father-in-law and those men who had served with him. If that is the case then he would surely have been given more detail by Agricola on what was probably a defining moment at the beginning of his Governorship. He has not recorded where he travelled from (Viroconium or Deva), what route he took, where this 'rebel' outpost lay... there are many hills in North Wales, and certainly which (and why he chose it) crossing point on the Menai Strait, who were these people that sued for peace, were they tribal leaders or Druids.... not even a tribal name is mentioned!. Something surely as significant as these would have been retained in his Agricola's memories and questions you thought Tacitus would have asked. It appears just a little too vague, but just enough detail to create a good impression of a prominent Roman and father-in-law in the history books.

As for the reality of the situation in the lands of the Ordovices and the other local tribes, 'peace' would now have prevailed in this region (along with the changes Agricola would institute in good politics, a fairer judicial and taxation system as well as administration changes) and of course a lot more forts and roman roads in the region manned by Auxiliaries[1] and Roman centurions controlling those roads and river crossings just in case!!

---

[1] *From AD 80 onwards Roman Auxiliary soldier numbers were equal to and later greater than Roman Legion troops; as the Legions were drawn back into Europe by successive Rome Emperors.*

The crossing of the Menai Strait at the onset of the winter months and the achieving of a peaceful resolution, should be seen as a master-stroke of tactics in his strategy against the resistance to Roman control of the province (and for Pax Romana in Britannia).

This second attack was not in fact a huge military affair but a clear and effective way of 'stamping' Rome's authority on the tribal leaders, an action of 'mind over body'. The very threat of Roman troops appearing in numbers without warning during the winter months meant that punitive action on them could occur at any time and in memory of the violence and destruction wrought on the island in AD 60... the tribal leaders would have been in no doubt after this that there was no 'safe time' now from Roman hostile military action.

Hostilities between the tribes of western Britannia and the Roman forces were at an end in the main as far as the classical texts record (the fact that both Frontius and Agricola installed a network of forts meant that they believed that they could still not trust the local tribes to keep the peace).

The campaigns in the west had taken a considerable amount of time, effort, and cost in men and materials to finally contain the western frontier. Yet little seems to have been made of this fact considering it was the end of a prolonged period of hostilities which had been ongoing since the time of Caratacus in AD 47, some 31 years before! Surely the longest active armed resistance of any tribes (other than the Silures) in Britannia against Rome; a fact that also seems to have little relevance in the history books of Britain. Boudicca appears to have more prominence for her short lived violent and bloody rebellion.

As far as Tacitus was concerned, the page of history was quickly turned to Agricola's next campaign, going North to deal with the tribes of Caledonia!!

What of Mona and the Druids post AD 78

It is clear from the texts that at some point prior to, or after the second attack on Mona that Governor Agricola realised that oppression was not the answer to gaining full control of, and obeyance from the Britannic tribes. He was probably aware that after the miltary actions of his predecessors peace was always short lived. The harshness of their rule had indeed incited acts of resistance to Roman authority.

It appears that Agricola was astute enough to realise that if he was to maintain a stable situation in Britannia he had to overhaul the Roman administration and do it quickly. As Tacitus records '*He (Agricola) determined to root out the causes of war. Beginning first with himself and his dependants, he kept his household under restraint, a thing as hard as many ruling a province. He transacted no public business through freedmen or slaves; no private leanings, no recommendations or entreaties of friends, moved him in the selection of centurions and soldiers, Trifling errors he treated with leniency, serious offences with severity. Nor was it always punishement, but far oftener penitence, which satisfied him, He lightened the exaction of corn and tribute by an equal distribution of burden, while he got rid of those contrivances for gain which were more intolerable than the tribute itself*' (reference to the Corn Requistion and the people compelled to deliver the corn to distant and sometimes inaccessible parts of the country and then pay inflated prices to buy it back again). His actions appear to have worked, there were no 'rebellious activities' recorded during his governship. He had learnt from the mistakes of his predecessors. He needed to ensure that the province did not have reason to rebel against the Roman establishment. Fair taxation, administration and justice should bring about a stable and peaceful province. It may also have been to stabilise the lands so that he could concentrate on his energies on his advance northwards into Caledonia.

Tacitus also makes a clear note of how the population was dealt with... *'in order that a population that was scattered and uncivilised and consequently ready for war, might become accustomed to peace and quiet he* (Agricola) *would assist communties to erect temples, market places and houses. Gradually the Britons went 'astray' in alluring vices; to promenade, bathe and enjoy well appointed dinner tables'.* Scattered communities were potentially a threat to Roman rule and difficult to control and tax. The key was to draw them into central projects were they could be influenced or maybe 'enamoured' by the benefits of what could be on offer or available to them to 'better' their lives. Civilisation it appears requires population centres with market and religious centres to promote trade in food and goods and the opportunities for wealth would eventually draw them away from the 'old ways'. Agricola also continued the promotion of education amongst the sons of tribal leaders and the elite in language, dress and lifestyle; an indoctrination into Roman ways and values! He was careful however and allowed them to retain their native religion as long as it did not act as a focus for rebellion.

His overall strategy appears to have been effective, certainly in the lowland zone of Britannia where there appears to have been a reduction of the number of active military fortlets in these areas (much of these would have been the source of his troops for his campaign against the northern border and Caledonia). It was easier in this richer agricultural zone inhabited by the most populous and politically advanced tribes who were very much tied to the land where their crops grew. Unlike the highland zones where the tribal homesteads would have been based either on the summer or winter pastures of the herds of animals spread throughout the hills and mountains. Production of food (both in crops and livestock) per hectare would have been much lower due to poor soil quality. Communities would have been been much smaller and spread out over greater areas only really coming together at market time to sell their produce.

Regarding the lands of the Ordovicians and its stability under Roman rule, the tribe appeared to have retained some autonomy but Agricola did establish more forts within the area. This included a significant Roman military fort at Segontium where a natural harbour on the Afon Seiont was easily accessed from the Menai Strait close to its SW entrance into the Hibernian (Irish) Sea.

Its position made it easy to be supplied by sea and it would probably have been a 'hub' fort (Casey and Davis 1993) making it easier to resupply the existing and new forts in the region rather than risking potential attacks on long overland supply routes from Viroconium and the east. As added security for the region a Legion fortress was also established at Deva with port facilities (which would become the major military centre of western Britannia).

From the current evidence we have there were no Civitas centres established in this northern region of the Brythoniaid (known as this until the 11th Century when the region we now know as Wales would be identified) so the establishment of these forts and infrastructure; the construction of connecting Roman roads linking them, clearly indicates that the Roman governors were still wary and these were a 'just in case' insurance that any rebellious activity could be deterred or dealt with quickly and not allowed to escalate. These tribes people were not going to be 'cowed under the Roman yoke' they appear to have been fiercely independent and solid in their own culture. Roman troops had shown that they could eventually defeat them in skirmishes and battles but recognised that they could not be controlled in the longer term without Roman military presence.

The classical texts regarding Mona are sparse after the incursion of Agicola. It appears that the lack of any notations regarding the island or the Druids in the texts of the Greek and Roman historians showed that were was little of any consequence happening there to put pen to paper, it was merely a backwater of the Roman Empire. Given this scenario the Celtic culture would have survived tenaciously in this region. Small spread out communities could not be so easily swayed by Roman ways. It would have been their way of continuing the resistance of Roman influence by maintaining their communal and cultural identity without taking up arms against them.

The fact that two Roman governors decided to attack Mona clearly indicates that they saw this island as a real problem with regard to Roman rule within Britannia. Both attacks were carried out in completeley different ways and led to different outcomes.

Paulinus decided that a ferocious and crushing blow should be meted out on the Druids and the 'resistance' but was interrupted and he had to leave to deal with the Boudicca rebellion in the south east. His conquering of Mona was not completed, his troops were taken away from the island, so it was seen to be only partially successful. It does begs the question as to what the tribal landscape of the island would have been if Boudicca had not raised a rebellion. As it was the 'resistance' was still alive when he left.

Agricola chose a rapid strike (with no apparent casualties on either side) when it was least expected by the islanders who were presumably totally unprepared and which led to a settled peace between the tribes and the Romans to such a level that the nearest Roman fort of any size was on the mainland at Segontium not on the island itself.

It is hard to believe that the resistance would have crumbled completely after Agricola's attack, it is more likely that an agreement was negotiated which basically said ' if you agree to us retaining the basic governance of our island we will cause no more trouble'. Agricola may well have agreed this and just for good measure ensured that the forts at Segontium and Deva were to continually manned by Roman troops (though at a latter date it is more likely that they were Auxiliary troops who had gained Roman citizenship). We know that on Mona at least two forts and a watchtower (Caer Gybi, the fort at Cemlyn and Caer Tŵr) were built in relatively close proximity to the sheltered bay and harbour on the NE side of Holy Island, but the archaeological dates for these range between the 1st and 3rd Century. There are also partial remains of a Roman structures at Llanedwen (2012 Gwynedd Archaelogical Trust). Their construction could have been a form of control of trade but also by the 3rd Century regular raids were being carried out against Mona by the Irish, Scotti (Scots) and Picts so it is likely these were constructed in response to these attacks.

Research struggled to find any specific information on the Druids on the island or the rest of the Ordovician lands during this period. They seem to have disappeared from the classical texts.

Had their influence been neutralised by the invasions of Mona, and therefore the Greek and Roman historians saw no relevance in mentioning them again? Or had the Paulinus invasion been so destructive that it had destroyed the very foundations of their society to a point where it was not possible for them to recover as cohesive part of Celtic society.

Those Druids and Druidessess who had survived or were located elsewhere at the time of the 'Destruction' on Mona would they have then wandered the land as prophets, seers, possibly councillors, 'doctors' of herbal remedies, custodians of ancestral heritage and lore, musicians and poets. Given that this region never really became 'romanised' it is far more likely that the various categories of Druids continued to be a part of the tribal society though Roman law and justice may well have superseded their role within the tribal system. They still had an important part to play within the society though eventually their influence would have diminished as those who had spent 20 years being trained by the 'teachers' on Mona died and there was no-one to replace them.

There are records held in the National Library of Wales dating to the 12th Century that mention Bards as still being in prominent positions in this society and their continued role in language, music and poetry. They were responsible for maintaining, updating and recounting the 'TRI CHOF YNYS BRYDAIN' – trans. as the '3 Records (or Memorials) of Britain':-

1st = The history of notable acts of the kings and princes of Brydain and Cambria

2nd = The language of the Brythains, to preserve the ancient tongue and not intermix it with any foreign or words to prejudice the true language.

3rd = The genealogies or descents of the nobility, their division of lands and their armies

Note: the tripartite system again? coincidence or continuation of an older culture?

What is different in this case is that these Bards were paid a stipend out of every ploughland in the country (western Britannia). In order to receive this every 3 years the Bard had to visit the houses of all the **gentlemen**[1] in the country (the visit was called the **CYLCH CLERA**- rough trans. is 'poet's circular journey') in order to preserve the TRI CHOF. At the first visit the Bard would collect all the memorable actions events and deeds of that house and land (its history). He would take note of the death of a 'great' person, his descendants and children, the division or portioning of the lands, and armies. The Bard would then receive a set stipend from the house. He then had to visit the house again three years later to collect any new information and add it to what he already had. This would be repeated every 3 years for the stipend to continue to be paid.

In the Llanstephan MS:144[2] *Anonymous (early 17th Century) there is a reference that translates as 'The Gentleman ot the Countrey had a special interest in the Tri Chof, for the Histories were the acts and deeds of their ancestors and kinsmen and the preservatione of the Language, Armies, descents and Divisione of lands were they owe proper service and therfor the Stipend payd by them to the Bards was notconstituted wythout good cause and reasone. And all the Histories and acts of Kings and nobility were collected by them all the Batells were recorded by them and expressly remembered voppon the* ***Cerdd foliant*** *(poems that laud and praise the gentleman or gentlewoman during their lifetime) of such noble persones as had performed the service in the feelde and vppon their* ***Cerdd farwnad*** (poems of lamentation of a gentleman's death after he has

[1] *The* **gentlemen** *were known as* **Gwr bonheddic** *in the Brythonic language and under their law they could only be called that if they were paternally descended from the 'Kings and Princes of Brythain'*

2 *MS (Manuscripts) held in the National Library of Wales*

deceased) *soe that there are noe mistakings of truth in setting down histories from three yeare to three yeare. There was a greate punishement inflicted by the lawe vppon the Bards wyth long imprisonment losse of place and diginitie wyth great disgrace if any should sett downe for truth but truth in any historical treatie whatsoever, for noe man dyd treate of any Batell but such as was an eyewitnessthereof for some of the cheefest of the Bards were the Marshalls of all Battels and of Cousell for directinge the field and the Kings or Generals Inteligences how the Batell went on, soe that they could not be ignorant of any passaige or thinge donne in field'.*

From this 17th Century manuscript it is clear that these Bards were the custodians of the tribal leaders history (not too dissimilar to the role of the Druidic Bards), which was recorded at or close to the time of these events. It also states that such events recorded by individuals were not accepted by law as they had not been witness or present at such events. Clearly truth was a key feature of this Celtic culture and this Tri Chof was a recognised and accepted form of proving ones deeds and ancestry. This knowledge was important in maintaining their status and even raising it within their society when accession to a higher position was being challenged. Far from being lost forever there are records that clearly show at least the Bards were still an important part of the society long after the Druid 'University' had been destroyed.

Given the lack of documentary evidence to the contrary it is likely that Druidic culture in all its forms did continue throughout the ages of the Roman occupation in the lower levels of the society and not by those who had been seduced by the offerings of the Roman culture.

Evidence that the Bards still played a prominent role amongst the Welsh nobility is signified by the presence of

the Bard Iolo Goch in Owain Glyndŵr's inner circle during the 14th and 15th century independence uprising against the English crown (as recorded by Iolo's patron Ithel ap Robert the Archdeacon of St Asaph).

The Druids did not build in stone, they used the natural landscapes of trees and stone features, so there is no physical evidence today that shows us of their existence, customs and rites on the island we now know as Anglesey/Ynys Môn or indeed in the rest of mountainous and forest of the Ordovician lands. With no written records either it is very difficult in either defining or interpreting the Druid cult activity in this region and therefore determining the reason why Rome sought to destroy them on Mona.

It is also true to say that this Brythonic region was not significant to the Romanisation of Britannia and is reflected by the fact that this part of Britannia contains almost no Roman religious buildings or temples, apart from where the Roman military was located (fortresses, forts and fortlets) reflected the very varied religious practices of both the Roman and Auxiliary soldiers evidenced by archaeological finds in the forts and surrounding area (possibly the site of a local vicus) e.g the cult of Mithras in Segontium.

As a quirk of fate the other religion that Rome had banned, Christianity, got a foothold initially in the lands of the Silures and Demetae in the 4th /5th Century AD and and moved northwards and was to have a significant influence on the land. The word 'Llan..' in Welsh place names denotes a religious site associated with both Celtic and Roman Christianity in Wales. An impact so many place names starting with *Llan* we can see in Wales today indicates how much of this 'one god' religion had on the region.

Note *Wales is believed to be derived from the Saxon term* ***Wealas*** *meaning 'foreigner'. The Saxons saw the Brythonic peoples of Western and Northern Britannia (which included Cornwall, Wales and Yr Hen Ogledd ('The Old North' encompassing northern England and the southern Scottish lowlands) as foreigners to their way of life. Pressure from the invaders advancing from the east (Saxons, Angles and Jutes) and north (Picts and Norsemen) between the 3rd and 7th Century shrank the lands occupied by them to a point where Cornwall and Wales became separate entities and some of the northerners of Yr Hen Ogledd came south into the land of the Wealas in western Britannia. It must be clearly stated that the term was not used to identify a country for at least a few hundred years (when the Angles/Saxons held sway in eastern Britann*ia).

There is also the term in the Brythonic language ***COMBROGI*** *meaning fellow countrymen. later evolving to* **CYMRU/KYMRY,** *those sharing the shared territory of Cymru*

It became more prominent from the 4th century AD onwards when it became the official religion of the Roman Empire. In AD 313 Emperor Constantine allowed Christians to worship without restriction (he converted to chritianity on his deathbed) and by AD 400 ALL other religions were been banned in the Roman Empire. The Celtic church established itself into the life of western Britannia and through time abandoned aspects of Roman Christianity. At the end of the 6th century Rome's head of the church, Pope Gregory I, dispatched a mission under the monk Augustine (later to become the first Bishop of Canterbury) to reassert papal authority over the Celtic Christians and bring them back within all the precepts of the Roman church. They refused and it would not until the Norman conquests that the Celtic Church came into the fold of the Papal authority as a single church of Roman Christianity.

Epilogue

The Roman invasion of Britannia was not just all out warfare. Indeed there were tribes who acquiesced to Roman rule preferring Rome to their more aggressive tribal neighbours. Bribery and the promise of no military action against others bought the tribes in as 'client kingdoms' as long as they showed no aggression to the Roman presence. The time line on page 39 shows the time period it took Roman governors to claim so much of southern and middle Britannia as theirs. The crushing defeat of the most powerful tribe in the south at this time, the Catavellauni, in AD 43 would have sent shock waves through the land; though its leader Caratacus[1] would lead a strong resistance further west with those who still considered the Romans invaders and must be challenged if not defeated.

It does appear from the strategies the Roman governors employed that their main aim appears to have been to gain control over the the lowlands of the south and midlands; those which would provide financial gain to Rome through grain, slaves and metals. The lands to the west and north could wait as these where more mountainous areas more difficult to 'conquer' and probably less profitable. It would also stretch their military resources possibly to breaking point.

After his defeat Caratacus[1] moved through the lands of the *Dobunni* (centred on the region around we now know as Gloucestershire) and into the land of the *Silures* of south east Wales. From here is believed to have led *Silures* and Ordovician attacks on Roman troops and their allies into the *Dobunni* region from AD 47. He had learned that Roman

---

[1] *He is recorded as Caratacus in the Latin texts of Tacitus*

troops could not be beaten in open battle but by guerilla 'hit and run' warfare which they proved to be very effective at and causing the Legion based in Glevum (Gloucester) serious problems from AD 47. Incursions by the Romans and the building of a fort inside Silurian lands forced Caratacus further north into Ordovician lands and they now began attacking not only the the *Dobunni* lands but also the *Cornovii* (who had also sided with Roman rule) to the north of the Dobunni. The Roman governor Ostorius Scapula went after Caratacus and his forces and eventually beat him at Caer Caradog in AD 50. Caratacus fled to the north for safety with the *Brigantes* and Queen Cartimandua. This defeat and the loss of their leader however did not stop the resistance, he had trained the tribes well in their tactics and they knew their lands well; the Roman troops had a fight on their hands. After the capture of Caratacus (Queen Cartimundua handed him over to the Romans as she was pro Roman) Scapula apparently turned his anger to finally defeating the *Silures* and *Ordovices* and publically vowed, as they posed such a danger, they should be annihilated as *'the Romans had done to the Sugambri of Gaul and blotted them out of existence'*. This public declaration inflamed the tribes and they increased their attacks on the Roman fort being constructed on their land and foraging parties.

Tacitus records in his Annals, 12.38
'Instantly they rushed from all parts on the camp prefect, and legionary cohorts left to establish fortified positions among the Silures, and had not speedy succour arrived from towns and fortresses in the neighbourhood, our forces would have been totally destroyed. Even as it was, the camp prefect, with eight centurions and the bravest of the soldiers were slain; and shorthly afterwards a foraging party of our men, with some cavalry squadrons sent to their support, was utterly routed.'

12.39
'Scapula then deployed his light cohorts, but even thus he did not stop the flight, till our legions sustained the brunt of the battle. Their strength equalized the conflict, which after a while was in our favour. The enemy fled with trifling loss, as the day was on the decline'.

It is not known whethere any Romans/Auxiliaries were captured and what their fate would have been. It was not only the declaration that had triggered this reaction; the Roman Auxiliary commanders had allowed their men to plunder indiscriminately during their military actions in the region; taking captives, seizing booty and behaving in an 'arrogant and high-handed' manner. Time and again the Roman authorities appear to not consider how far they could push these tribes and were the surprised by animosity building up against them. The resistance was going to continue with the Silures at the forefront.

When Scapula died in the winter of AD 52 the *Silures* were still very active. His replacement Aulus Didius Gallus was hastily sent find the XX Legion (under Manilius Valens had been heavily defeated in their actions against the *Silures*, so he withdrew what was left of the Legion back to Glevum where he apparently combined forces from the XX and the X1111 and went on to annex the lands of the *Demetae* (whose lands lay on the western border of the *Silures*). Rather than go directly against the tribe he then appears to just quell any incidents and concentrats on building more roads and forts in the borderlands to contain the tribe.

His replacement arrives in AD 57. Quintas Veranius Nepos revises the previous policy and begins military operations against the Silures with the XX moved back to the fort on the river Usk, but he dies within the year. There is no record as to whether he has successfully subdued the tribe.

With this in mind it raises the question as to why Paulinus chose to attack the Ordovicians and Mona when the greatest problem appeared to be the *Silures* who were still very active against Roman troops on his arrival in Britannia. There are no records of military action or incursions by the Ordovices during this whole period, neither is there any mention of Druids causing problems amongst the local population. Yet it is they and the island of MONA INSULIS that see the full wrath of the Roman military machine fall upon them to near total annihilation in AD 60. Was the attack by Agricola in AD 78 purely about the attack on the Roman auxiliary cavalry units in Ordovician lands or was there more to it on Mona.

As a final point, the resistance of the *Silures* lasted until after Sextus Julius Frontius (Governor and military strategist from AD 74-77) began serious military incursions into the Silures uplands. It was never made clear as to whether it was a clear defeat over them or that both sides came in to an 'understanding', their resistance has lasted for some 25 years longer than any other tribe so far since the invasion. Yet this fact and their guerilla action prowess has been overshadowed by the events of the death of the Druids on MONA and the Boudican revolt.

Of the Druids little is known of those that survived, perhaps they became doctors, upholders of laws and justice within the tribes or perhaps as hermits living in isolated groves continuing to practice their rites and science. Their culture and lore dwindling to history as centre of learning had been destroyed. As for the Ovates could they have been drawn eventually to the new religion of Christianity as it began to flourish in the 3rd century. The Bards we know did continue as poets and even at the time of Owain Glyndŵr in the 14/15th century a Bard named Iolo Goch composed poems for him and many other nobles.

Mona would see more attacks and destruction from raiders over the next few centuries but men from 'the old north' (Yr Hen Ogledd) would come and settle on the island (at Aberffraw) and create the Royal House of Gwynedd, whose descendants would become so influential in the history of the country that would become Wales. Two of its sons **Cadwallon** (who died in battle near Hadrian's Wall in AD 634) and his son **Cadwaladr ap Cadwallon** were considered to be the last **two High Kings of Britain.** Mona and it leaders would face many attacks from differing foes that would take the island to the brink but resistance was embedded in its very soil. Even later the island would be the ancestral home (Penmynydd) of the most powerful dynasty on the English throne, the **Tudors.**

Had the Druids whom the Romans appear to have feared so much left something deep in the heart of the island so that future generations would flourish as leaders of a resistance against tyranny from outsiders?

Rome had been startled by the Druids use of immolation of human prisoners as a form of punishment, yet in Rome such prisoners were placed in an arena and torn to shreds by wild animal for the entertainment of its citizens. Which was the most 'barbaric'?

One final thought...

The curses and incantations that the Druids railed out against the Roman troops as they landed on the shores of Mona, where they really aimed at that wall of steel that they could not possibly break or where they meant for further afield? Paulinus's assault on the Druid island was halted because the tribes of the south-east of Britannia had risen up against Rome and were on the rampage destroying all that was Roman. The insult to Boudicca and her daughters by the Roman Procurator was the start of it but very rapidly ten of thousands of differing tribes who until that point had not united against Rome joined in the destruction. Had those curses reached out that far to drive the rebels to attack Rome's weakest spot not only to destroy the Romans but also avenge the destruction of Mona. The rebels chose to destroy the heart of 'Rome' in Britannia, Camulodunum and the Temple of Claudius with fire just as Paulinus has done with the Druids sacred groves on Mona. Had the Druids had their revenge or was this just a just coincidence and the rebels had seen an opportunity when they saw the weakness of the Roman military strength in the region when Paulinus had taken his best troops to Mona?

Roman Emperors and Governors of 1st Century AD Britannia

Emperors		*Governors*	
AD		AD	
41 – 54	Claudius	43 – 47	Aulus Plautius
		47 – 52	Ostorius Scapula
		52 – 57	Aulus Didius
54 – 68	Nero	57 – 58	Quintas Veranius Nepos
		58 – 61	Gaius Seutonius Paulinus
		61 – 63	Petronius Turpilianus
68 – 69	Galba	63 – 69	Marcus Trebellius Maximus
		69 – 71	Vettius Bollanus
69	Otho		‘
69	Aulus Vitellius		‘
69 – 79	Vespasian	71 – 74	Quintas Petillius Cerealis
		74 – 77	Sextus Julius Frontius
		77 – 84	Gaius Julius Agricola
79 – 81	Titus		‘
81 – 96	Domitian		‘

Classical Text Sources

Caesar Julius: 100-44 BC, Roman general and dictator.
He recorded first-hand his account of his battles, actions and observations during his invasion of Gaul (mainly France and Belgium) and Britannia between 58 and 50 BC. His book 'Commentarii de Bello Gallico' was written in three parts and amounted to 8 books in total (Book 8 was completed after his death by Aulus Hitius who had served as his legate during the campaign).

Josephus: AD 37- circa 93, Jewish historian.
He recorded the history of the Jewish Revolt against Rome which began in AD 66. His works are believed to be some of the best descriptions of the Roman Army as a military machine.

Pliny The Elder: AD 23/24 -79, Roman historian.
Born in Como, Italy, he was a Roman naval and army commander who was also a prolific author on subjects such as philosophy, natural history and geography.

Cassius Dio: AD 155 – 235, Roman historian of Greek origin.
After over two decades of research he wrote 80 volumes from the foundation of ancient Rome to AD 229. Books 56 60 cover the period from AD 9 – 54 and the death of Emperor Claudius.

Diodorus Siculus: 90-30 BC, Greek historian.
He wrote the Bibliotheca Historica consisting of 40 books, many of which have not survived. They did reach the period of Julius Caesar and the Gallic wars (circa 60 BC)

and with some very clear descriptions of the Gauls and the land of Britannia, Book 5 chapter 19-38.

Pomponius Mela: AD 15-?, Roman geographer of Spanish origin.
He wrote DE SITU ORBIS around AD 43. A work of three books in which he described the national characteristics and scenery in the lands around the Mediterranean. He clearly documented the customs of a variety of tribes and specific groups including the Druids which do not appear in other classical texts.

Strabo: 63 BC-23 AD, Greek geographer and historian.
Travelled widely around the Mediterranean. His seventeen books in the 'Geogrophica' covers all the main provinces of Roman Empire and their social, cultural, economic and geography; including Britannia and the islands around it.

Seutonius Tranquillus: circa AD 69 – AD 126?, Roman historian.
He was a friend of Pliny the Younger, who helped him to gain positions in Rome with Emperors Trajan and Hadrian. He wrote a complete works on the Roman Emperors from Julius Caesar to Domitian called 'The Lives of theTwelve Caesars'.

Publius Cornelius Tacitus: AD 56 – 120, Roman historian.
His two main works that cover the Roman Empire were the Annals covering AD 14-68 (though Books 7, 8, 9, 10 and the beginning of Book 11 covering the years AD 37 to AD 47 are missing) and Histories covering AD 69 to 96. He aslo wrote extensively about his son-in-law Agricola. Of all the classical texts it was from these writings that historians gained their information about Rome's impact on 1st century Britannia.

Gildas (Gildas Sapiens): AD 500-570.
A monk who trained in a monastery in Glamorgan before travelling to Brittany. His **'De Excidio et Conquestu Britanniae'** *trans. From Latin as* 'On the Ruin and Conquest of Britain' c. AD 540 which recounts the history of the Britons before and during the arrival of the Anglo-Saxons. It is strongly critical of Kings and leaders of that time. His information sources are identified but no longer exist. **Nenius:** a 9th century welsh monk based in Powys but little is known of his life. He is credited with the authorship of **'Historia Brittonum'** *trans. from Latin as* **'The History of the Britons'** c. AD 830. The work is believed to be a compilation of texts from various sources (including Gildas). Though it has been seen as inaccurate; events, people and places not always matching, it does give a good indication of the life of the times and includes events associated with the Picts, Scotii, Vortigern and the Arthurian legend (which Geoffrey on Monmouth would expand upon in his work 'Historia Regum Britanniae' - History of the Kings of Britain)

Annales Cambriae *trans, from Latin* **'The Annals of Wales'**. Circa 10th century. It is a compliation of Welsh/Latin texts drawn together at St Davids in Dyfed. Again many of the sources no longer exist. Though it mainly covers events in Wales it does also cover events in Ireland, Scotland and England.

Trioedd Ynys Prydein *trans, from Welsh as* **'The Triads of the Island of Britain'** and also known as the Welsh Triads. Circa 12th/13th century. They are a collection of medieval manuscripts written in groups of three that recount persons, events and places in Welsh history. They are recorded in such a way that suggest they may well have been the memories of the Tri Chof Bards: differences in names, places and events could be accounted for on this premis. There are also elements of these in the Llyfr Gwyn Rhydderch (the White Book of Rhydderch), the Llyfr Coch Hergest (the Red Book of Hergest) and the Llyfr Du Caerfryrddin (the Black Book of Caermarthen) the earliest, important and notable manuscripts written in the Welsh language. Many of which would be included in the contemporary book the Mabinogion: the earliest stories in the literature of Britain based on earlier oral traditions.

Brut Y Tywysogion *trans.from Welsh a*s **'Chronicle of Princes'**. Antiquary Robert Vaughan (c.1592-1667) was a collector of old manuscripts. The collection was known as the Hengwrt-Peniarth Library which is now held in the National Library of Wales (in Aberystwyth). There were a number of versions translated from the original Latin (which does not now exist). The most important version of Brut Y Tywsogion is the Peniarth MS20 and covers the period from AD 682 and ends in AD 1332 and is classed as one of the major sources of Welsh history.

Giraldus Cambrensis (Gerald of Wales) AD 1146-1223. Archdeacon of Brecon who accompanied the Archbishop of Canterbury, Baldwin of Forde, on a tour of Wales in 1188. His account of that journey, was recorded in his ***'Descripto Cambriae'*** in 1194. This work was a treatise on all aspects of Wales and its people. The geography, its principalities, their way of life including their music and bardic poetry. It is a valuable historical document as a snapshot of Wales during this period.

References

Bédoyere, Guy de la: *Roman Britain A New History*, Revised Ed. 2013. Thames and Hudson.

Breese, D J: *Roman Forts in Britain*, 2002. Shire Publications

Coppens, P: *Anglesey: Druids's Island.* 2002, Original article appeared in the Frontier Magazine 8.1.

Dando-Collins, S: *Legions of Rome – The Definitive History of Every Imperial Roman Legion*, 2010. Quercus

Davies, John: *The Story of Wales*, 1993. Allen Lane, Penguin Pressure

Encyclopedia Britannica: *Anglesey*, 1911 Edition

Frere, Sheppard: *Britannia: A History of Roman Britain* 3rd Ed. 1987. Routledge and Kegan

Gildas: De *Excidio Britanniae* (On the Ruin of Britain) 6th Century, *trans* by J A Giles, Serenity Publishers, 2009

Gower, John: *The Story of Wales*, 2012. BBC Books

Gregory, Donald: *Wales Before 1066*, 2008. Gwasg Carreg Gwalch

Hanson, W S: *Agricola and the Conquest of the North*, 1987. B T Batsford Ltd

Harvey, J G: *The Flow of Water through the Menai Strait*, 1968. Geophysical Journal International, Vol 15, Issue 5

Hassall, M W C: *Batavians and the Roman Conquest of Britain*, 1970. Britannia Journal Article, Vol 1

Jones, J Graham: *The History of Wales*, 1990. University of Wales Press

Jones, Rebecca H: *Roman Camps in Britain*, 2012. Amberley Publishing

Kaye, Steve: *Roman Marching Camps In Britain*: GIS Statistical Analysis and Hydrological Examination of Known Camp Sites, Resulting in the Prediction of

Possible Camp Sites, 2013. www.babdaarcgeophysics.co.uk

Kaye, Steve: Observations on Marching Roman Legionaires: Velocities, Energy Expenditure, Column Formations and Distances. 2013. www.babdaarcgeophysics.co.uk

Kendrick, T D: *Druids and Druidism*, 2003. Dover Publications

Lloyd, D M and E M: *A Book of Wales*, 1969. Collins

Matyszak, P: *Legionary*, 2018. Thames and Hudson

Miles, D: *The Tribes of Britain*, 2006. Weidenfeld and Nicholson

Monmouth, G: *The History of the Kings of Britain*. Trans. by Lewis Thorpe,1966. Penguin Classics

Moorhead S and Stuttard D: *The Romans Who Shaped Britain*, 2012. Thames and Hudson

Oliver, Neil: *A History of Ancient Britain*, 2011 Weidenfeld and Nicholson Nenius: *Historia Brittonum* (History of the Britons) 9th Century, trans. By J.A. Giles

Roberts, Alice: *The Celts*, 2015. Heron Books

Ross, Anne: *Druids Preachers of Immortality*, 1999. Tempus

Roth, J.P : *The Logistics of the Roman Army at War* (264 B.C – A.D.235),1999, Brill

Rowlands, Reverend Henry: *Mona Antiqua Restaurata: An Archaeological Discourse of the Antiquites, Natural and Historical of the Isle of Anglesey, the Antient Seat of British Druids*, 1723. Posthumously Revised 2nd version by Dr Henry Owen, 1766

Senior, Michael: *Anglesey: The Island's Story*, 2013. Gwsag Carreg Gwalch

Senior, Michael: *Hillforts of Northern Wales*, 2005. Gwsag Carreg Gwalch

Seutinious: *The Twelve Caesars*, Trans. 2007. Penguin Books

Tacitus, C: *Dialogus Agricola Germania*, Trans.1914. Heinemann (Loeb Library)

OS Maps:
Landranger 114: Anglesey / Ynys Môn
Landranger 115: Snowdonia / Yr Wyddfa
Landranger 116: Denbigh / Colwyn Bay
Landranger 125: Bala and Lake Vyrnwy / Y Bala a Llyn Efyrnwy

OS Historical Maps: Ancient Britain and Roman Britain

OS Maps housed in National Library of Scotland:-
Anglesey. Sheet XXIII. NW / Caernarfonshire. Sheet XI. NW pub. 1888
Anglesey. Sheet XX II.SE / Caernarfonshire. Sheet X. SE pub. 1888
Anglesey. Sheey XXIII. SW / Caernarfonshire. Sheet XI. SW pub. 1888
Anglesey. Sheet XXII. NE 2nd Edition pub.1901

Ancient Sites on Mona and the Adjacent Mainland, Contemporary to the Pre and Roman period of 43 to 78 AD

Stone walled hill fort/hut groups.

Caer Tŵr (p.193, 218)
Dinas (Menai Strait) -(p.151)
Dinas Gynfor (p.211) – see map
Dinas Dinorwig (p.66, 148, 149) – see map
Din Llugwy (p.208)
Caer Seiont (Caernarfon) (p.148)
Din Silwy/ Brwdd Arthur (p.207, 209)
Dinas Dinlle (p.66, 67)
Parciau (p.207)
Twyn-y-Parc -see map
Iron Age Huts on Holyhead Mountain (p.194)

Earthwork Enclosures with Banks and Ditches

Burial Chambers/Mounds and Standing Stones

Glossary

Place Names

Roman	***Today***
Aquae Sulis (p.59, 61, 196)	Bath
Burrium (p.61)	Burrium Gate
Brannogenium (p.65)	Leintwardine
Calleva Atrebatum (p.60)	Silchester
Camulodunum (p.48, 49, 56, 60, 87, 100, 182, 229)	Colchester
Canovium (p.48, 147)	Caerhun
Circucium (p.191)	Brecon Gaer
Deva (p.66, 98, 125, 190, 191, 212, 216, 218)	Chester
Ganganorum Prom (p.66)	Llŷn Peninsula
Glevum (p.46, 48, 49, 52, 55, 61, 97 112, 182, 189, 197, 225, 226)	Gloucester
Isca Silurum (p.191)	Caerleon
Letocetum (p.48, 97)	Wall
Levobrinta (p.191)	Forden Gaer
Lindum (p.42)	Lincoln
Manduessedum (p.57, 97)	Mancetter
Mediomanum (p.191)	Caersws
Novimagus Reginorum (p.60)	Chichester
Pennocrucium (p.48, 97)	Water Easton
Ratae Corieltauvarum (p.60)	Leicester
Segontium (p.146, 148, 191, 216, 218, 222)	Caernarfon
Venta Belgarum (p.60)	Winchester
Verulamium (p.31, 60)	St Albans
Viroconium (p.56, 57, 61, 62, 93, 97, 111, 117, 123, 125, 126, 128, 129, 137, 138, 140, 183, 189, 201, 212, 216)	Wroxeter
Vxacona (p.97)	Redhill